Prayer
in the
Workaday World

Just as there are three elements in man,
so there are three main degrees of prayer:

Oral or bodily prayer
Prayer of the mind
Prayer of the heart
(or 'of the mind in the heart', spiritual prayer)

Summarising this threefold distinction, Theophan observes:

*You must pray not only with words but with the mind,
and not only with the mind but with the heart, so that
the mind understands and sees clearly what is said
in words, and the heart feels what the mind is
thinking. All these combined together constitute real
prayer, and if any of them are absent your prayer
is either not perfect, or is not prayer at all.*

Igumen Chariton of Valamo, *The Art of Prayer,*
An Orthodox Anthology .

For the Community of the Resurrection

Prayer
in the
Workaday World

Arthur Middleton

GRACEWING

First published in 2007 by

Gracewing
2 Southern Avenue,
Leominster
Herefordshire HR6 0QF

All rights reserved. No part of this publication may be reproduced, stored in a retrieval system, or transmitted in any form, or by any means, electronic, mechanical, photocopying, recording or otherwise, without the written permission of the publisher.

© Arthur Middleton 2007

The right of Arthur Middleton to be identified as the author of this work has been asserted in accordance with the Copyright, Designs and Patents Act 1988.

Cover picture © Newcastle Libraries & Information Service

ISBN 0 85244 677 2
978 0 85244 677 5

Typeset by Action Publishing Technology Ltd,
Gloucester GL1 5SR

Contents

The quotations on p. i are taken from *The Art of Prayer, An Orthodox Anthology*, compiled by Igumen Chariton of Valamo (E. Kadloubovsky and E. M. Palmer (trs)), London and Boston Faber and Faber, 1978.

Foreword

When I was chaplain of Keble College, Oxford, I once invited a priest who had a distinguished and justified reputation as a teacher of Christian prayer to come and preach in the College Chapel. Afterwards there was an animated discussion with a group of students, in the course of which a young woman student pressed the question, 'But how *do* you pray?' Back came the answer: 'O, it is very simple, you only have two choices, you either start where you are, or you start where you are not.' He then went on to explain that starting where you are, meant starting with your feelings, your mood, your current joys and sorrows, the people to whom you are most closely bound, the causes which you have at heart. Starting where you are not, meant starting with this time of the Christian Year, the passages of Scripture or the Psalms set in the lectionary for the day, which might in no way match mood or feelings, but which could well challenge and inspire in new and unsuspecting ways. We all need, he said, both starting points – for our praying is enabled at the point of the engagement of the particularity of our circumstances and personality with the energy, grace and life of the Holy Spirit, who shapes us into the likeness of Christ, that we, as the beloved in the Beloved, may be enfolded by the Father's love.

In this book, which is both down to earth and practical, and, at the same time deeply rooted in the prayed experience of Christians down the ages, Arthur Middleton has provided a trustworthy guide and a real encouragement to the practice of the presence of God. This is tried and tested wisdom, and this enables the necessary judgements and discriminations to be made about much that passes in today's Church as 'spirituality.' The judicious comments about the use and abuse of Retreats in the appendix is particularly valuable here. If there has been in the past criticism of writing on prayer that it is so heavenly-minded that it is of no earthly use, this emphatically does not apply to this book. As an experienced retreat conductor and spiritual guide over many years, Arthur Middleton brings out of his treasury things old and new, and it is a welcome relief to read a book on Christian praying so rooted in the Christian tradition – the Fathers, the great spiritual writers of the Middle Ages, the Anglican seventeenth-century divines and the Tractarians and their successors – and which is yet so properly practical as to how to go about the business of praying, both personally and corporately. Arthur Middleton's gift of writing with exemplary lucidity and theological profundity has served him well in what he has offered to us in this book. Rooted in the Trinitarian life of God which lies at the heart of the Church's being, we have here a real resource for the renewal of Christian life today. Priests will learn from it, ordinands will profit by it, but above all every baptised Christian will find here words which will enable them to grow deeper in their faith, and to be shaped more fully in that holiness which flows from what St Paul called the great mystery, 'Christ in you, the hope of glory'.

   I commend this book most warmly, and pray that it will indeed bear fruit in the renewal of the life of prayer, not only in the Church of England, but more widely.

+GEOFFREY GIBRALTAR
Feast of St Clare of Assisi and obit of John Henry
Newman, 11 August, 2006

Preface

As a choirboy of ten I came under the influence of The Community of the Resurrection during a parish mission conducted by Fr Bell. It was an unforgettable experience, not least my spell of duty pumping the organ during the Mission Services. The Children's Mission was conducted by Fr Hoey who was then a novice. He encouraged us to have a special place in our bedroom marked by a crucifix, a candle, a religious picture and our prayer book and card. This would be our prayer corner and he would come along during the mission and bless it, which he did. Thereafter, the dressing table where this was focused developed a cross on the mirror, for which there may be a perfectly natural explanation, though it did seem strange. Anglicans have always had a certain kind of reserve about such overt expressions of religious devotion, yet in Europe and the East the inclusion of such a place for devotion within the domestic scene is common. The Children's Mission ended with the making of a resolution on a special card. Mine was 'to try to say my prayers more regularly', which was then signed by Fr Hoey, and then it went into the family Bible on the Prayer Corner.

That was the beginning of my association with the Community of the Resurrection that inspired me to take prayer seriously and learn its form and language from devotional manuals, now in short supply, and from the Church's Liturgy. It has continued throughout my life in the Fraternity, Commemoration Days, and Annual Retreats that were a lifeline for a parish priest, in the hours spent before the Blessed Sacrament in the Resurrection Chapel and in the worship of the Community, where the libera-

tion of South Africa began. So I dedicate this book to the
Community for what God has given to me through them,
as I continue to pray for more vocations to the Religious
Life.

When Eric Abbot, the former Dean of Westminster, was
appointed Dean of King's College London, he was told
that above all he must teach the ordinands to pray. His
weekly lectures on prayer were always well attended and
much appreciated. This was continued by his successor
Canon Sidney Evans and in the final year at St Boniface
College, Warminster, Canon John Townroe introduced us
to the Christian Mystical Tradition. Here I learned to do
theology, in the phrase of Michael Ramsey, 'to the sound
of church bells' and where the College Chapel was obliga-
tory and central to college life. This was just before some
people began writing their misinterpretations of Bonhoef-
fer's catchphrase 'religionless Christianity' and the rather
confused book, *Honest to God*, which with similar subsequent publications had such a destructive effect on the
well tried classical disciplines of Christian living, that
ushered in the madness of the sixties. So I am eternally
grateful to such college tutors, parish priests and spiritual
directors who have nurtured my way of Christian living,
and given me a standard by which to critically evaluate the
chaos and confusion that has been inflicted on the
Church, and at times by the Church, in the last forty years
or more. It is our association with such people who give
prayer a high priority in their lives that inspires our own
vision and affects our own life and practice of prayer.

This has enabled me to respond to invitations to address
matters of prayer, among many other contemporary theological issues to priests and laity, students, institutions and
individuals, not only across this country, but also in the
wider Anglican Communion across Canada and Australia.
So the substance of what I have written has been tried out
with audiences in Lectures, Retreats, Quiet Days, and
Schools of Prayer and published articles here and abroad.
At a time when senior churchmen are calling for a more
prayerful and a less talkative and activist Church, my aim
is to provide some vision of where to begin, how to
proceed, and how our prayer can continue to grow and

deepen. Hopefully, it will give people such a sense of prayer that the noise before the Sunday Eucharist in so many of our parish churches may begin to subside into the necessary prayerful stillness that the celebration of the liturgy requires. I have tried to be reader-friendly by keeping references and footnotes to a minimum. The need for practical application has been a priority throughout, to forestall the laity's criticism of those clergy who are always exhorting them to pray but never tell them how to do it. The aim of Part Two is to give specific guidelines on this level.

In a time of New Age ideologies and practices we need to avoid participating in phoney events that would pass themselves off as Christian and are no more than a scientism of mind control that the uninformed may accept as authentic. Appendix 1 addresses some of these matters in relation to the use and abuse of retreats.

A serious life of prayer must affect and change how we live; there are ethical consequences because the life of prayer is about becoming a new creature. It is not for the cultivating within us of the 'feel good factor' or to give ourselves a 'transcendental kick', which so often is associated today with the modern word 'spirituality'. We must apply ourselves to the practice of the virtues and realise that we cannot continue to live in the same old ways where these conflict with spiritual values. In short, we have to come to terms with sin, and unless we are prepared to let go of attitudes, resentments, negative memories that prevent reconciliation with those to whom we refuse to speak or relate, and habitual sinful behaviour, there will be no progress in prayer. Appendix 2 in Part Three addresses these matters.

Finally, as an authentic life of prayer begins to grow and deepen, there will come a time when a person will need a spiritual director. Hopefully, if a parish priest finds such a task not possible another priest may be suggested.

Part One
On Prayer

1

Treasure in the Backyard

The gift, which we have received from Jesus Christ in holy Baptism, is not destroyed but is only buried as a treasure in the ground. And both common sense and gratitude demand that we should take good care to unearth this treasure and bring it to light. This can be done in two ways. The gift of baptism is revealed first of all by a painstaking fulfilment of the commandments; the more we carry these out, the more clearly the gift shines upon us in its true splendour and brilliance. Secondly, it comes to light and is revealed through the continual invocation of the Lord Jesus, or by unceasing remembrance of God, which is one and the same thing. The first method is powerful but the second is more so, so much so that even fidelity to the commandments receives its full strength from prayer. For this reason, if we truly desire to bring to flower the seed of grace that is hidden within us, we should hasten to acquire the habit of this exercise of the heart, and always practise this prayer within it, without any image or form, until it warms our mind and inflames our soul with an inexpressible love towards God and men.

St Gregory of Sinai

If you want a life of prayer the way to get it is by praying. To pray is to share in God's life, to participate in the life the Father lives with the Son in the Holy Spirit. St Augustine said that God is nearer to us than the air we breathe. What makes him seem absent is that our awareness of Him is dulled and distracted, and this sense of God's absence prompts us to assume that the treasure of a living experience and knowledge of God lies in some 'far country'; outside the backyard of one's life

The story of the poor Rabbi in Cracow illustrates this point. He dreamed there was treasure buried under the bridge in front of the royal palace in Prague and set off to try and acquire it. He found the bridge heavily guarded but after some days chatted-up one of the guards and told him of his dream. 'Why', said the guard, 'you are a fool! Only last night I dreamed about a Rabbi in Cracow, looking very much like you, who had treasure buried in his own backyard. But you don't think I'd be fool enough to set off for Cracow in search of it.'[1]

The treasure we seek is in our own backyard, the real and living circumstances of life in the workaday world. We find that treasure as we respond to the spiritual fullness of life as it is, not as we imagine it to be or as we would like it to be. An early Christian mystic, St Isaac the Syrian, said that we must enter eagerly into the treasure house that is within us and there we will see the things that are in heaven. The ladder that leads to the Kingdom is hidden within our soul.

Prayer in the workaday world

Prayer must be intimately connected with life and is not to be a special segment of it, otherwise it would be false prayer. When it becomes an optional extra, it creates its own unnatural strain in not being integrated with the rest of life, and that is when many people stop praying. Life is the backyard in which is discovered the Light, Life and Love of God's presence, when prayer is allowed to spring up spontaneously in the pressures of living and thinking. The nature of one's backyard will determine the nature of

[1] A. M. Allchin, *The World is a Wedding*, London, Darton, Longman and Todd, 1978, p. 24.

one's prayer. If one's backyard is not a monastery or a vicarage, then one must not try to order one's prayer as if it were. St Francis de Sales makes this point in *The Devout Life*.[2] As in creation when God commanded the plants to bring forth their fruits, each after its own kind, so does he command all Christians who are the living plants of the Church, to bring forth the fruits of devotion, each according to his character and vocation and not according to anyone else's. The mistake St Francis warns against will lead to the desperation and the despair of a blind alley. The gentleman, the workman, the servant, the prince, the widow, the maid and the married woman, must exercise devotion in different ways. Not only this, but the practice of devotion must also be adapted to the strength, the employment and duties, of each in particular.

> ... is it fit that a bishop should lead the solitary life of a Carthusian or that married people should lay up no greater store of goods than a Capuchin? If a tradesman were to remain the whole day in church, like a member of a religious order, or were a religious continually exposed to encounter difficulties in the service of his neighbour as a bishop is, would not such devotion be ridiculous, unorganised and insupportable? Nevertheless the fault is very common.

Our backyard has many similarities to one's neighbour but it has also many differences. People are different in temperament, some are married, and others are single, so that the detail and framework of daily life is not always the same. All these facts of life affect people in different ways, and must be taken into account when working out how prayer is to be practised in our lives. It is fatal to slavishly follow someone else, and though another person's experience may be a guideline, our prayer must be related to the circumstances of our own lives. We must begin with ourselves in the real situation of life as it is now. It follows that while accepting the same principles that must form the basis of every life of prayer, there will be similarities of operation but also differences of opera-

---

[2] *The Devout Life*, Francis de Sales, London, New York, Toronto, Longmans, Green & Co., 1953, p. 7.

tion as these principles are woven into the fabric of different lives.

Most people's backyard is the workaday world that centres around the hopes and trials of home and family and at work, whatever the job. Here is where the treasure will be found as we come to know and experience the presence of God as the Lord of all life. Here we discover how worship and life, work and prayer, help to uncover and reveal more of the treasure of God's Presence. In this backyard we meet with the mystery of God when we turn the whole of life in his direction. St Ambrose describes the experience like this:

> If the soul desires it, if it prays, prays unremittingly and without hesitation, reaching out undividedly to the Word, suddenly it seems to hear the voice of Him, whom it does not see and recognises the fragrance of his divinity in the depths of its being – a thing which many experience who rightly believe. The nostrils of the soul are suddenly filled with spiritual grace, and it feels itself to be breathing the air of His Presence whom it seeks and it says, 'So this is He, whom I seek, whom I desire!' Does it not happen that when we are pondering something in the Scriptures and cannot find the explanation, in our questioning, in our very seeking, suddenly the highest mysteries appear to us.[3]

The desire for prayer

To repeat, people are different. These differences affect people in their desire for a life of prayer, and must be taken into account when working out how prayer is to be practiced in our own particular circumstances. We need to pray as and how we can. Nevertheless, what is essential and common to all is a *holy desire* for a life of prayer, which is nothing less than a longing for God. In chapter five of her *Revelations,* Julian of Norwich describes it like this:

> God showed me too the pleasure it gives Him, when a simple soul comes to Him, openly, sincerely, and genuinely. It seems to me when I ponder this revelation, that when the Holy

---

[3.] Psalm 118, *Sermon,* 6.8–9; *Patrologia Latina,* 15 col. 1337.

Spirit touches the soul it longs for God rather like this; 'God of your goodness give me youself, for you are sufficient for me. I cannot properly ask anything less, to be worthy of you. If I were to ask less I should always be in want. In you alone do I have all'.

St Augustine of Hippo said,

The whole life of a Christian man is an holy desire. What you long for, as yet you do not see ... by withholding the vision, God extends the longing, through the longing he extends the soul, by extending it He makes room in it ... so brethren, let us long, because we are to be filled ... that is our life, to be exercised by longing.

2

Communal Prayer

But, of course, the symbol of the Kingdom par excellence, the one that fufils all other symbols ... as well as the whole of the Christian life 'hidden with Christ in God', (Col. 3:3) is the Eucharist – the sacrament of the coming of the risen Lord, of our meeting and communion with Him 'at His table in His Kingdom' (Luke 22:30). Secretly, unseen by the world, 'the doors being shut', the Church that 'little flock' to whom it was – the 'Father's good will to give ... the Kingdom' (Luke 12:32) – fulfils in the Eucharist her ascension and entrance into the light and joy and triumph of the Kingdom. And we can say without any exaggeration, that it was from this totally unique and incomparable experience, from this fully realized symbol, that the whole of the Christian lex orandi *was born and developed. ...*

Alexander Schmemann

Not alone

Our pilgrimage towards participation in God is not a flight of the alone to the Alone. We journey with others, fellow-members of the worshipping community of Christ's Body. Here, in the communal worship of the whole Body the Christian's life of prayer begins, by joining 'in the apostles' teaching and fellowship, the breaking of bread and the prayers' (Acts 2:42). We must consciously and deliberately root our own praying in the Church's prayer, joining the praying Church by going to church. Baptism initiated us into the life of communion with God, making us a member of Christ by the power of the Holy Spirit, so that being a Christian means that I belong to something much bigger than myself. By virtue of the life Christ lives in me, I am identified in real fellowship and communion with fellow members of the Body of Christ. Thereby is Christian life communal by nature and relationship with God is mediated through membership of the Church, so that our praying is part of the prayer of the Church, resting upon the praying Church and being part of it. The primary concern is to join together in common prayer, where Word and Sacrament becomes our manna from heaven. The heavenly manna is fed into our hearts and minds in the hearing of the Word of God, and into our mouths by feeding on the Bread of eternal life. In drinking the Cup of Salvation, our lives are nourished by Word and Sacrament within the community of salvation in the way of salvation. So our pilgrimage in prayer must be set within the community of faith where we share in the common task of seeking God. Celebrating the Eucharist, the Resurrection of the Lord, Sunday by Sunday, secures that the rest of the week is lived in the power of the Risen Christ. The Church's liturgy is a school, where we catch something of the essence of prayer that becomes powerful in the realm of personal prayer, as it places our prayer in the larger context of the Church's prayer. There can be no serious life of prayer if we neglect participation in the communal prayer of the whole Church.

The Eucharist

In gathering to celebrate the Eucharist the Church demonstrates itself most truly as the Body of Christ, and is constituted as such by the Eucharist. In this action, what is foretold in Scripture is fulfilled before our very eyes, as Word and Sacrament, Scripture and Eucharist, are wedded together to lead us into an experience of salvation, saving life. The Liturgy becomes the epiphany or manifestation of New Life, the sacrament of Christ's coming and presence where God communicates himself personally in his sanctifying power. Here on the Lord's Day, the first day of the new creation, rooted in the resurrection of Christ, Christ, the Life and Light of men comes into the midst of his own at the weekly Easter. The First Day is also the Eighth, because to partake of the life of God is to participate in that which is beyond time. So the Eighth Day becomes the figure of life everlasting, the symbol of eternity in which we now live because of Christ. Therefore it is the day without evening, the last day, because no other day can follow eternity.

The Eucharist makes the Church the Body of Christ and the Temple of the Holy Spirit, a realm of grace, a communion of persons living in the life that Christ shares with the Father in the Holy Spirit. As each feast and liturgical season takes us through the Christian Year, to remind us of the events and plan of our salvation from Advent to Pentecost, the Lord is present and the desire for God is renewed in our hearts and lives. The place where we gather to celebrate the Eucharist becomes a House of God and the gate of heaven, where Christ becomes for us that mysterious ladder in Jacob's dream, the meeting place of heaven and earth. Here the Christian focuses all of his life, expressing himself most truly as a child of God and is seen by others most truly for what he is. Here he expresses his faith in God, commemorates and participates in God's work of salvation, and then expresses and applies that salvation to the whole of human life. In the bread and wine offered, the people offer their life and work as 'All things come of you, and of your own do we give you.'

The Christian must handle life in exactly the same way that Jesus handled life. He handled life and his Father's gifts in the same way in which he handled that bread, because his identity and destiny were bound up with that piece of bread. Of such identification, he could say as he took it, gave thanks for it, blessed it, broke it and gave it, 'This bread is Me; it is my life I am giving to you; from now on it is to be your life; this bread is what life is all about'. This bread makes us a Christophoros, a Christbearer or a Theophoros, a Godbearer, a living Eucharist of the divine presence. 'We are the Body of Christ', to be taken in exactly the same way as that bread was taken, that we might be consecrated, broken, and shared out to be a means of grace, a vehicle of the divine life from whom all things come. The Body of Jesus is to be discerned in the life of his people.

'We are the Body of Christ.' In the life of his people Jesus is to be recognised in actions that speak louder than words. We are the people in whom the action of taking, blessing, breaking, and giving, is really to be demonstrated. Our destiny is interwoven with this divine pattern in that piece of bread. This is our life, as it was Christ's life, whose body we now are. What is done in Jesus and in that bread has to be done in us, as we offer ourselves to 'be taken, blessed, broken and given'. The shape of life is Eucharistic, and our witness is to demonstrate that this is what life is all about. This is God's pattern, the shape in which he offers us saving life, because Christ has died, Christ is Risen, Christ will come again. In the Liturgy Christ gives himself to us. The Liturgy takes place on earth, but it belongs to the realm of heavenly realities and was not instituted by a human being or an angel, but by the Spirit himself, so that those who are still living in the flesh should think of performing the service of angels.

> O what mercy, O what love of God for human beings! Christ who is seated with the Father in highest heaven is at that moment grasped by the hands of all and does not hesitate to give himself to anyone who wants to embrace him and be bound to him. He, whom the eyes of faith perceive is possessed by everyone.
>
> You remember how Elijah was surrounded by a great crowd and had in front of him the victim for sacrifice placed on the stone. [cf. 1 Kgs. 18] Everyone stood stock still. The silence was complete. Only the prophet raised a prayer. Suddenly, from heaven came down fire on the victim. It was a marvellous spectacle that filled everyone with amazement. Here, however, something much more than a marvellous spectacle is unfolded. Something is happening that is greater than any marvel. Here the priest draws down not fire but the Holy Spirit himself.[1]

---

[1] John Chrysostom, *On Priesthood*, 3,4; *Patrologia Graeca,* 48, 642.

Consecration of all life

Participation in the Eucharist brings a whole new attitude to life and to others, as it forms us in the attitude of Christ. From now on our vision of the world around us in the chaos and confusion of its struggles for justice and peace, the problems of environment, peace and race, of wages and just rewards, of international terrorism, will have within its perception a perspective that is not of this world. For the life we now live in Christ is for better and for worse, for richer and for poorer, in sickness and in health, in time and for eternity, till death us do part.

Sunday-by-Sunday Christians celebrate the Eucharist, the Resurrection of the Lord, not to forget about the rest of the week but to secure that the other six days are lived in the power of the Risen Christ and according to his will. This principle has always been at the heart of Christian worship and life. Whether Paul or Peter, Barnabas in his missionary wanderings, the countless others in market or field, slavery or persecution, they could all dedicate every moment and work to God in the power of the resurrection life, because of times apart each week for the worship of God and the reception of that life.

This principle finds its greatest expression in the sacramental life of the Church, where the sacraments are not enclaves into which the Christian escapes from the rest of life because he thinks such life is empty of God. It is through the sacraments that the rest of life is consecrated. From the presence of Christ given in the Eucharist, the consciousness and experience of that presence informs every moment. It is not merely a matter of offering to God special times set apart for prayer, or of making all we do into a prayer. By setting apart certain times specifically for prayer, we consecrate the whole of what we do to God. Our times of prayer focus the prayer that is the offering of our daily work.

Go and serve the Lord

'Go in peace to love and serve the Lord' is not a cosy way to round off a nice service. It is the sending out of God's servants to do what God wants us to do in the workaday world. Out we go from the common prayer of the whole community. The Christian's prayer is part of the praying of the whole Body, so that personal prayer will naturally and rightly be affected by our experience of such common prayer as personal prayer becomes quite unconsciously clothed in the kind of language used in church. This was the experience of Staretz Silouan. He was a Russian peasant who became a monk on Mount Athos and became one of the greatest men of prayer in the twentieth century. His education was limited to two terms in a village school, and so he found that much of the language and inspiration of his personal prayer came from the Liturgy that was such a regular and familiar part of his monastic life. He clothed his own prayer in its language. Look at the *Private Devotions* of that seventeenth-century Anglican bishop Lancelot Andrewes, or Archbishop Laud, and you will find that they learned the language of prayer from the prayers of the Church and they demonstrate that there is a language of prayer to be learned.

The intention and language used in common prayer and worship can be woven into our own personal prayer. In this way we begin to pray in the spirit of the whole Body, which gathers into itself the experience of the ancient saints, contemporary fellow-members, the martyrs and confessors of previous ages. Our own personal prayer needs to be caught up into such a rich and diverse experience; the prayer of God's people through the ages. It will take us beyond the parochialism of our own personal experience and prayer, bringing a vision of the height, depth, and width of relationship God allows us to have with him.

This relationship expresses itself in acknowledging that God is holy and that the earth is full of his *glory,* in Eucharistic Thanksgiving, the supplication of intercession and litany, and in the reality of mystery and symbol, as we participate in sacramental acts. A relationship of this kind engages the whole person in the adoration that loses itself in wonder, love and praise, prompting our gratitude to him from whom all good things come. But it also moves to contrition and repentance in order to experience the joy

of healing in forgiveness. Then do we feel able to bring the
needs of other people into his presence and at the same
time request him to supply our own need.

The liturgy is a school, where we catch something of the
essence of prayer that becomes powerful in the realm of
personal prayer, as our own more formal approach to God
in personal prayer becomes all the more significant. We
begin to see it as part of the prayer that the whole creation
addresses to its Creator. Being already 'in Christ', a limb of
that Body whose Head is the Lord Jesus our own praying
becomes more intimate. Through Jesus Christ Our Lord,
we are sharing in that intimate communion of life that
Jesus lives with the Father in the Holy Spirit. Living in this
communion of life, the divine milieu, we can approach the
throne of grace and communicate with the King of Kings
as Master and Lord, but also as friend to friend.

Liturgical and personal prayer

Participation in liturgical prayer fosters ways of acting as
responses to prayer and influences the way one prays
outside the Liturgy. In the Christian Mystical Tradition
there is no dichotomy or conflict between Liturgy and
personal prayer, for they are two aspects of the Christian's
praying which are essentially mutually inclusive. In his
Contemplative Prayer Thomas Merton sees this conflict
between 'public' and 'private' prayer as a 'modern
pseudo-problem'. 'Liturgy by its very nature' he says,
'tends to prolong itself in individual contemplative prayer
and mental prayer in its turn disposes us for, and seeks
fulfilment in, liturgical worship.'[2] In the 1960s Michael
Ramsey wrote:

> Liturgical movements strive to bridge the gap between
> worship and the common life, and just now they gather to
> themselves much enthusiasm and romance. But will these
> movements succeed unless there is with them a revival of

[2.] Thomas Merton, *Contemplative Prayer*, London, Darton, Longman
and Todd, 1973, p. 55.

contemplative prayer? There are signs, not perhaps many, but enough to be significant, of a new discovery of contemplative prayer in the setting of everyday life. Contemplative prayer is the hunger and thirst, of desire for God ... Such is the prayer that links Christianity and ordinary life.[3]

Liturgical and spiritual renewal is inter-related and there can be no emergence of effective worship until both kinds of renewal are taken to heart.

Nathan Mitchell underlines this inter-relationship, pointing out that personal prayer explodes into the speech of public praise and sacramental action, while the speech of worship erupts into the still point of silence where, as T. S. Eliot says, 'there is only the dance'. The prayer of the heart structures the experience of worship while worship shapes the content of personal prayer. This implies the need to penetrate beneath the outward trappings to the essence of liturgy, that we might comprehend its inner meaning and implications as we give liturgical worship a place in the life of the soul. Such an understanding and appreciation of the experience of liturgy will increase our awareness of what kind of personal prayer can be derived from it, and how one's conduct and life choices should be shaped by it. A delicate balance is required between liturgy as a unique experience of God in common prayer and as a means for ordering one's personal devotion, An appropriate response is required by, and derived from, the celebration of the Liturgy, and the whole aim of liturgical renewal has been to reunite liturgy with the devotional life of all Christians. Discovering this harmony between the experience of liturgical prayer and the rest of one's personal devotion brings a level of integration. Common prayer and personal prayer are interdependent and there should be no antipathy between them. While common prayer gives depth and width to personal prayer, in its turn personal prayer gives the kind of life that prevents common prayer from becoming mechanical.

Dogma, prayer, and life, all three have been isolated; and in

[3.] Michael Ramsey, *Sacred and Secular*, London, Longmans, 1965, p. 57.

isolation their power and glory have vanished and withered away. The Church, if it is to win the fight against modern paganism, and not only win the fight but heal the wounds inflicted by this paganism on man's nature, needs re-integration, a new wholeness, in which the dogma, the prayer and the life form a living unity ... it has failed to find any point of contact where dogma, prayer, and life all meet, any one definite action which is the meeting-place of eternal truth, and the sweat and toil of humanity. Man needs to see such an action, which will not only integrate his working life into the eternal world, but also give him a vision of what working life should truly be.[4]

[4] G. W. O. Addleshaw, *The High Church Tradition*, London, Faber and Faber, 1951, p. 18.

3
Prayer and Time

Prayer must not be simply an occupation for a certain time, but a permanent state of the spirit. 'Make sure', says St John Chrysostom, 'that you do not limit your prayer merely to a particular part of the day. Turn to prayer at any time, as the Apostle says in another place: "Pray without ceasing" (1 Thess. 5:17) ...' I remember that St Basil the Great solved the question how the apostles could pray without ceasing, in this way: 'in everything they did', he replied, 'they thought of God and lived in constant devotion to Him'. This spiritual state was their unceasing prayer.

Bishop Theophan

The mixed life

Today some of the new conditions in which people have to live, such as noise, rush, activism and lack of privacy, make it difficult to pray. It produces strain, a continual nervous restlessness and too many entertaining diversions. Also, there is the undue pressure put on people by the cult of efficiency. Taken together with the high-pressure commercialism and the go-getting of the West, people find the atmosphere in which they have to live charged with tension. They end up so distracted, that their common complaint is that there is no time to pray within the quickened pace of life, and the changes that have altered the pattern of life. Yet, increasing numbers of people want to pray. Finding a way to pray will mean discovering a measure of independence and mastery

within the new conditions of life. It is possible to continue
one's ordinary life and make very little change, at least in
the outward circumstances, but it will require a determined stand against the disintegrating distractions in
order to secure the necessary time for prayer. A way of
doing this is to adopt the Christian principle of the 'mixed
life' in which prayer and action are blended. St Augustine
advocated this way of prayerful living to Christians in his
day, and St Gregory the Great, who lived in distracted and
violent times, preached to mixed congregations on the
merits of blending prayer and life.

The primary aim is to maintain the prayerfulness of the
whole of life, a prayerful stillness in which one is
conscious of God's Presence when life in the workaday
world is buzzing with distraction. There are people whose
excuse for not going to church is that they can worship
God anywhere. In reality they end up worshipping God
nowhere. Some practising Christians claim that they need
no set times for prayer because they can pray anywhere at
any time. Brother Lawrence is cited to support this attitude which misses the secret of Brother Lawrence's
example, who was able to maintain the prayerfulness of
the whole day because he spent seven times a day on his
knees in the monastery chapel. Only then was he able to
find God in the pots and pans of life. Without the spirit
and principle of that kind of discipline, not the pattern,
one risks ending up by not praying at all.

Going about one's work in shop, factory, school and
office with vague religious sentiments, is completely
different from the person who stands at his factory bench,
convinced that his work is part of his prayer whereby he
partakes of the priesthood of Christ. That person is
consciously expressing the unity that exists between work
and prayer. Pious thoughts and sentiments are not always
prayer. The offering of one's work and everyone whom
one meets is only possible because of specific times for
quiet and prayer. In Christ, every act is a communion with
and worship of the Father. His life illustrated that it is not
a matter of 'times for prayer' or 'prayer at all times'. The
times of prayer make it possible to pray all the time.

Planned prayer

The ideal of the 'mixed life' is not something new; it is very ancient. Gregory the Great, the pastoral Pope who often preached about it to mixed congregations in Rome's churches, did so because it was part of the rich Christian tradition of prayer. Here we stand on very old ground, searching for treasure that was once currency, but has long been buried and is forgotten by most people. The ideal of the 'mixed life' is adaptable and flexible and therefore it is able to meet the various needs of those aspiring to a serious life of prayer. People who put a great deal into life receive a great deal from it, and they are able to do so because they meet the demands of their time and fit many things into their day. A South African farmer comes to mind. His day began early and this for him was the best time to pray. It began with five minutes every morning but after several years he was getting up two hours earlier for his prayer. I think of a husband and wife who rise at six for an hour's prayer, Bible reading and silence.

One is not suggesting this pattern for everyone, but the spirit and principle needs to be grasped in the lives of those who aspire to a serious life of prayer, because what is true of life is true of prayer. Those who plan their prayer are those who put most into it and get most out of it. A simple experience can illustrate this. In packing the boot of a car there must be some system; otherwise there will not be sufficient room for everything. Pack it systematically and its surprising what can be packed into it. It is like that with Time. If there is some plan then all sorts of things can be fitted in. One of these will be the opportunity for prayer provided there is the desire to find a place for it. Then like meal times we will find ourselves missing our times of prayer only very rarely.

Other factors in planning prayer

Temperament and feelings are important considerations that must not be overlooked when planning prayer. Some people pray better in the evening than in the early morning. As a student I noticed this in two of my tutors. Both were men of prayer, but one would be in chapel late into the night while the other was there very early in the morning long before the Eucharist. They found the best time for their sustained prayer and planned it accordingly, having good reason for being different. There may of course, be bad reasons, but that does not matter provided a person is faithful and is able to deal with his feelings. A powerful aid is an accepted plan that tells a person that though he may be preoccupied and his feelings are not congenial to prayer, if he does not pray now it will be missed out altogether. Despite his feelings he gets on with prayer and discovers how a plan can help with the good and bad elements of one's feelings.

As my tutors illustrated, people are different, and if prayer has an intimate connection with life, then we will bring our personal differences and peculiarities into our prayer. Just as in life we have our likes and dislikes, so in prayer we shall find ourselves having personal preferences about different kinds of prayer. Some people feel that they must always be praying for others, or for causes, and that this is the only authentic kind of prayer. Others want to spend their time just thinking about God, this is called meditation. People are at different stages in the life of prayer, which is only to be expected, so the secret is to keep moving and not remain in one place because one prefers it to anywhere else. A serious life of prayer needs a balanced diet, otherwise one's spiritual life becomes unbalanced and unhealthy and even stagnates. Planning one's prayer assures a balanced approach and saves one from being at the mercy of one's natural inclinations, one's likes and dislikes.

Dangers of planned prayer

There are dangers attaching to organised and planned prayer, but this is no reason to abandon something worthwhile. Recognise the dangers and strive to overcome them, reducing them to a minimum. There are three such dangers to be avoided.

First, there is a danger when playing with systems. Some people love to play with systems and end up attaching more importance to the plan than to the prayer. Prayer is much more than an ordered system of time and words; it is a life rather than a technique and the life must take precedence over the rule. The plan is only an aid. So if a particular plan does not help a person to pray, then it should be scrapped and replaced with one that is more useful and helpful. Before doing that, get on with praying and let experience test the worth of any plan.

Secondly, a plan can kill spontaneity. This is avoided by refusing to be rigid in sticking to one's rule of only praying at set times. The purpose of set times is to help maintain the prayerfulness of the whole day at home, work, or in the pub. I remember someone who was enslaved by a rigid routine. It prevented him from going out on Friday night because it was bath night, which also prevented him from having a bath on Thursday or Saturday night. If prayer is a personal relationship there must be spontaneity that prompts one to pray easily at any time of the day or night. The more one prays according to a plan, the more natural it becomes to pray at any other time.

Thirdly, the demon pride is never far away. The Pharisees thought that their fulfilment of certain religious observances and obligations made them better than anyone else. The classic parable of the Pharisee and the Publican highlights this. So beware of false comparisons with others and their plan or lack of a plan. The plan should become one's secret discipline, necessary for such weak creatures as ourselves, whose desire is to travel the straight and narrow road of prayer. Planned prayer is not a status symbol but an identity mark of spiritual immaturity in which is wrapped a life hidden with Christ in God.

Time and prayer[1]

To many people time is an uncontrollable element that brings fortune and misfortune into their lives. For the

---

[1.] For some of these insights on 'Time' I am indebted to Theodor Bovet, *Have time and be Free*, A. J. Ungersma (tr), London, SPCK, 1965.

Christian, God controls the future, therefore 'all things work together for good' (Romans 8:28) and because 'You are my God, my time is in your hand'. There is more to time than minutes and seconds, months and years. It is a precious and priceless gift from God in which to fulfil life's purpose by serving him and our fellowmen. Therefore it is our moment of opportunity, moving like an ever-rolling stream, each moment passing beyond recall.

When seen as a sacred trust time becomes valuable and we begin to use it wisely. 'Redeeming the time', means quite simply using it to the best advantage. Within it there is always an element of uncertainty, the 'ups and downs' of life, which even after seventy years seem as yesterday. The present is the only moment in our control, because the past has gone and the future has not yet arrived. 'Now is the accepted time, today is the day of salvation', meaning that the present is the moment of opportunity when we must 'seek the Lord, while he may be found'. Watch therefore and accept your time, a period of grace God gives us that we might realise life's purpose. Then and only then does it become life's most priceless possession.

Today's materialism has given time a monetary value and when it is identified with labour it becomes ludicrously overpriced. Such over-evaluation stimulates panicky anxiety lest time is lost. Drivers stopped at the traffic lights and shoppers delayed in long queues at supermarket checkouts are often tense with such anxiety. An automated atmosphere creates the illusion of time as some kind of empty space into which we must pack as much as possible. This attitude is completely wrong. 'Time is much more a manner of living that is mysteriously granted to us. It flows along in its particular rhythm, then again it mysteriously ceases and is transmuted into eternal life.' Life is much more than a set of aims and objectives to ensure what needs to be done, nor is it simply a habitual practice of doing things on the spur of the moment. There is more to it than mere quantity, because it has a qualitative value that is best explained like this. Suppose a person asks how long will it be before the potatoes are ready for harvesting; the answer will depend on when the question is asked, in the spring or the autumn. A simple answer about the quantity of time it will take cannot be given. Similarly, our day has a particular structure, so the duration of a particular job depends on the moment it was begun and more often than not it takes longer than anticipated.

Another illustration can help. After a heavy meal certain types of work are difficult to accomplish, yet early in the morning the same work is so easy. Mental 'barren' times are especially suited for more mechanical work or just pottering about. This is to discern in a qualitative way how best time can be used. Such sensitive discernment can decide the best time for certain occupations of the day, the times for prayer and work, the best disposition to do this and not that. Such a discerning use of time will accomplish the tasks in better and shorter time. Time has its own living rhythm, and the occupations of our lives, in so far as we are able, should be organised to suit it, because it cannot be arbitrarily divided. It has height, depth, breadth and its own peculiar and change of colouring. Our lives must be experienced as a harmonious wholeness in relation to this kind of time and then we will be able to discern the appropriate moment for each particular task.

Time belongs to God

Time measured by our clocks is not a full and correct conception of actual time. We must think of it in terms of the personal structure of each existing life. God gives it. The New Testament understands it in terms of the decisive moment of time, the God-given moment. 'My time is at hand' says Jesus. Life presents prominent moments in which certain works can be accomplished. 'Now is the accepted time', means that time is the opportunity given us by God, that we can grasp, or be like Jerusalem and 'fail to know the time of your visitation'. Hence, it is not our own time we choose to arrange for ourselves, but the commanded opportunity, a definite step in God's plan of salvation for mankind. This lays on us an urgency to seize the given opportunity, the concrete situation God puts us into, the time of the specific moment in which God expresses his will to us. If we do not listen now, at once, the opportunity will quickly pass us by. In this way God shapes the time of our life.

Between people who love each other there is a wordless communication. The sleeping mother still has an instinctive ear for her child asleep in another room, and is awakened from sleep when the child is disturbed or in need. Similarly, the husband who loves his wife knows immediately by her disposition and the look in her eyes when she is tired. Communication of this kind exists between people who love each other. We can also experience it with Christ if we love him with all our heart. Then our ear, an interior sensitivity, would be permanently tuned in his direction so that we would perceive his voice among all the discordant voices of the world around us.

If we have the conviction that Christ is the Lord of our time, that he has a definite design for each day as well as for our entire life, and that this expresses itself in a series of time's distinctive moments, the rest will follow. We will really become calm and listen within ourselves and learn what he desires from us in this moment and that moment or in this decision for today. Prayer helps us to grow into such a disposition and focuses our vision with a perspective that is not of this world.

4

Deciding Priorities

Rising early in the morning, stand as firmly as possible before God in your heart, as you offer your morning prayers; and then go to the work apportioned to you by God, without withdrawing from Him in your feelings and consciousness. In this way you will do your work with the powers of your soul and body, but in your mind and heart you will remain with God.

Bishop Theophan

The mixed life

The ideal of the 'mixed life' assists in the finding of an appropriate moment for the tasks that need to be done, and this includes discovering the appropriate moment that can be given entirely to God. It is essential to be practical and recognise our real limitations in order to make the best use of the possibilities available. Two considerations are vital at this stage. First, at all costs the quality of prayer must be preserved and it may have to be done at the expense of quantity. Secondly, we will need a balanced 'diet' of prayer that includes the various elements of adoration, thanksgiving, contrition and intercession. Avoid the temptation to pick congenial bits, because that will lead not only to a very inadequate idea of prayer, but also to a very inadequate idea of God.

Begin the day with prayer. Whether the morning is a good time for sustained prayer will depend on the person, their temperament, metabolism and circumstances, so that the appropriateness of the morning can vary from one person to another. When meals have to be prepared, buses or trains caught, and a clock-in deadline to be kept, the time for sustained prayer will be later in the day. However, acknowledgement of God's presence at the beginning of the day is essential. This can be brief, expressed in a simple dedication of the day to God, the Lord's Prayer, and a thanksgiving for the present day's life. Conclude with a brief prayer of commendation of the day to God, a brief prayer for guidance and direction, and a prayer for those with whom one will be living and working during the day.

Though the morning is often a time of rush, it can be a time of prayer as one moves from bedroom to bathroom, shower to make-up or shaving soap. A better way, if this is possible, is to spend ten minutes just being still. Most people know how long it takes from getting out of bed to arriving at work. Add another ten minutes into the calculations and set the alarm for the appropriate time. Pray before or after washing, just kneeling or standing in the bedroom at the spot that has become identified as the place of prayer, before a cross, crucifix, or icon.

The Book of Common Prayer, *The Alternative Service Book*, or *Common Worship*, which can be used privately, can be of help. Use some of the canticles and prayers from these books. Here are some suggestions.

1. Praise God

Begin by saying a canticle, varying it each day:

The Venite	Sunday
The Jubilate	Monday
Easter Anthems	Tuesday
Benedictus	Wednesday
Great and Wonderful	Thursday
Saviour of the World	Friday
Gloria in Excelsis	Saturday

2. *Thank God*

Almighty and everlasting Father,
We thank you that you have brought us safely
      to the beginning of this day.
      Keep us from falling into sin
      Or running into danger,
      Order us in all our doings;
      And guide us to do always
      What is right in your eyes;
      Through Jesus Christ our Lord.

3. *The Lord's Prayer*

4. *Collect for Easter 4*

Almighty God,
who alone can bring order
to the unruly wills and passions of sinful men:
give us grace
to love what you command
and to desire what you promise,
that in all the changes and chances of this world,
our hearts may surely there be fixed
where lasting joys are to be found;
through Jesus Christ our Lord.

5. *Prayer for Guidance*

Eternal God and Father
You create us by your power
And redeem us by your love:
Guide and strengthen us by your Spirit,
That we may give ourselves in love and service
To one another and to you;
Through Jesus Christ our Lord.

6. *The Grace*

During the day

As the day begins most people become involved very quickly with the many tasks that press upon them in the workaday world. This brief dedication to God at the beginning of the day may well produce offshoots during the day and these may come at certain identifiable times and places. The Spirit in which the day is begun will inform the prayerfulness of the whole day and become the spirit in which it is lived. The aim is not to encourage pious poses at the factory bench, or in the office, but to encourage the finding of times during the working day when a person, without loss of concentration on work and without anyone being aware of it, can say quietly a familiar prayer.

Such moments may come when clocking-in at the factory, or at the start of the day in office or shop, before or after morning break, or at lunchtime. A person will need to discover his own moments when he can do this. Such prayerfulness inculcates a spirit of worship and dependence on God and makes prayer something easily offered during work. Uniting prayer and work in this way makes it the daily offering to God. Prayer then ceases to be something exclusively associated with Sunday, crisis situations and those times when we consciously kneel down to pray. All life's experiences are seen to provide opportunities or seeds for prayer, and this spirit of prayerfulness enables people to be aware and see God in those parts of the workaday world where hitherto he had seemed absent. As we allow ourselves to be involved with God in his Creation, in the raw materials of daily work and relationships with people, we discover God inviting us to participate with him in the life of his world. In factory and office, shop and pub, we begin to discover and understand something of Brother Lawrence's experience, as we find, see, and know God, among the 'pots and pans' of life in the workaday world.

This experience is what saves the person who prays from the schizophrenia that separates prayer and work, and insulates us from the world in which coal is mined and candyfloss is made. Devotion is not extra to life but the spirit in which life is lived, so when we pray there is something quite simple that we must remember. Here and now the heart, which we open to God, is the point at which not only our personalities but the whole complex of relationships to things and people, is open to his touch and presence and thereby to his power to order and redeem.

In the evening
Prayer at night is an essential part of the daily routine. Again it will depend on the considerations noted earlier, whether it is the time for something short or something sustained. If the evening is not a time for sustained prayer, then an appropriate time must be found, when in a more relaxed atmosphere more time and attention can be given. It may not be possible to find such an appropriate time every day so it may have to be on alternate days or twice a week.

Evenings are the time for socialising, watching television, interior decorating or night class, a time to fit in things that cannot be done during the working day. Inevitably, people are usually very tired when they go to bed. This makes it difficult to pray for any length of time so that earlier in the evening will be a better time, perhaps after the evening meal, when its effects have subsided, or about nine o' clock. It would be good, if at a pre-arranged time each evening or on certain evenings of the week, the television could be switched off and for the next half hour husband and wife might pray or read the Bible together. Such a slot of time could be flexible according to the circumstances of the evening. It may be that like the couple who go to bed at a reasonable time in order to rise early to pray, others will find some time during the evening for sustained prayer. There can be no life of prayer without the discipline of the will.

Again, the Church's prayer books can be useful. If Adoration and Thanksgiving have formed the main diet of prayer in the morning, the evening can include the other elements of prayer, such as Penitence, Intercession and Petition. Here are some suggestions:-

1. Recollection

Personalise such prayers in this way:
Father, I come into your presence to hear and receive your holy word, to bring before you the needs of the world, to ask forgiveness of my sins, and to seek your grace, that through your Son Jesus Christ, I may give myself to your service.

2. Penitence

Say slowly and deliberately
If we say we have no sin we deceive ourselves and the truth is not in us. If we confess our sins, God is faithful and just, and will forgive us our sins, and cleanse us from all unrighteousness.
   Then be quiet and still reflecting on your sins as you mention them to God in your own words.

Follow with this prayer, personalising it
Almighty God, our heavenly Father, I have sinned against you and against others, in thought and word and deed, through negligence, through weakness, through my own deliberate fault, I am truly sorry and repent of all my sins. For the sake of your Son Jesus Christ, who died for me, forgive me all that is past; and grant that I may serve you in newness of life; to the glory of your name. Amen.

Then use the prayer of absolution, again personalising it
Almighty God,
who forgives all who truly repent, have mercy upon me,
pardon and deliver me from all my sins,
confirm and strengthen me in all goodness, and keep me in life eternal;
through Jesus Christ our Lord. Amen.

3. The Magnificat and The Lord's Prayer

Mary's song of praise and the Lord's Prayer can lead from Penitence into Intercession.

4. *Intercession and Thanksgiving*

A loose and flexible scheme can assist one into an informed and intelligent prayer for others. The calendar in our prayer books can be a resource for informed intercession, with its Saints Days, Ember Days, Rogation Days and Special Days of Intercession and Thanksgiving. A Subject Index of Prayers for Various Occasions can provide the basis of one's own personal scheme and some useful prayers. Using the Collect for the day in one's daily prayer brings personal prayer into the larger dimension of the whole Body in which one's personal prayer must always be rooted (see the Practical Suggestion in Part Two).

5. *Bible Reading*

The evening is often the best time to include a regular bible reading. It may take the form of a psalm, an Old Testament or New Testament reading. The Church's daily lections can be used to give it some point and pattern. They can be helpful in providing a daily reading that follows a systematic course. A saint's day can provide readings for that particular day.

Flexibility

A pattern of prayer can never be rigid. Flexibility is necessary to maintain the principle when the pattern has to be changed. Life can be so busy that some people may find it impossible to secure time and quiet for prayer every day. A mother with young children or an aged relative to care for, a doctor when the pressure of work is unavoidably great, or a man on night shift finding that life is all bed and work. Such situations can make the keeping of a plan impossible. Nevertheless, if there is a proper flexibility, the fundamental principle of the 'mixed life' is maintained, quick adjustment can be made so that opportunities might be grasped in the unexpected gaps of a crowded day.

Another worthwhile consideration is the safeguarding of a weekly withdrawal for prayer and reading when daily withdrawal becomes impossible. The arrangement of the week's timetable might well give priority to such a commitment and become the oasis that makes the life of prayer just possible. The cumulative effect of what might seem a minimum commitment to prayer may just enable people in such difficult circumstances to keep spiritually alive, while maintaining the prayerfulness of those circumstances that otherwise overwhelm them.

Finally, there are a number of people whose circumstances make it possible for them to give more time to prayer than they imagined possible. People living alone can be encouraged to use their solitude to pursue a more serious life of prayer that will lead them into the discovery that while loneliness is a prison, solitude opens up endless vistas when they can become aware of a presence that God spontaneously shares. Solitude is not found so much by looking outside the boundaries of your backyard, but by staying within. Solitude is not something you must hope for in the future. It is a deepening of the present, and unless you look for it in the present you will never find it.

Such people can be encouraged to say the shorter form of the Offices for Morning and Evening Prayer that are readily available today. A useful book of offices is the shorter version of *Celebrating Common Prayer,* from the Society of St Francis, or from the Community of the Resurrection *A Week of Simple Offices.* The homes of such solitaries in our urban deserts might well begin to blossom as cells of prayer, sustaining the life and witness of the whole body of the faithful. I well remember a good Christian woman, very human but not pious, whose doctor husband was a devout Parsee. Every night she said Compline after some spiritual reading. At the age of fifty she discovered that she had systemic schlerosis. A year later she died, a few moments after saying Compline and reading her nightly passage from Julian of Norwich's *Revelations of Divine Love.*

It may be that our standards concerning a serious life of prayer are far too low today and many are being called to aim higher. A wise and experienced spiritual guide has written: 'Many Christians give two hours each day to prayer; I do not think that you can follow our Lord as a disciple with less than one.'

Prayer and life

Prayer and life are not separate compartments of experience, because prayer is the living way of knowing and experiencing God in the daily circumstances of life. Not only will it require familiarity with many kinds of words, but also the need to discern and listen to things we have never heard before. God will speak to us through our lives. So often in life God brings to our notice a matter that needs attention, either for the first time, or repeatedly, so that we might see it more closely or in a different way. If we fail or refuse to respond to what we should when we should, we may well be stuck in one place for half a lifetime.

It is important to realise that prayer and life will not always develop in the same progression as they do in our logical consideration of them. Technical books on prayer may give this impression, though without intention. Experience demonstrates that some of the features that might be expected to appear at the end might well show signs of appearing at the beginning and vice-versa. Genuine prayer is bound into, and affected by, the rest of life as it actually is, so that it is not possible to set one's life in order first and then begin to pray. One begins to pray and from it follows the vision that indicates where life needs changing, making any progress in prayer dependent upon changing what needs to be changed. The greater the progress in the life of prayer, the greater will be the adjustments in the life we live, so that keeping one's feet firmly on the ground of one's own backyard is essential. From here everything in one's life must grow and enable one to find the courage to discover one's own modest and true way.

Always remember it is the Holy Spirit who leads and teaches us in the way of prayer at every stage of our pilgrimage. Response to the Holy Spirit depends on a willingness and readiness to be changed by the deepening and growing relationship that develops. This formation in the Spirit is not self-evident. It is mysterious, shaping and forming a person in a way known only to itself, involving the entire perspective of God's grace and the supernatural virtues whereby we are given a share in the divine life.

Prayer liberates the capacity and potential for such life, enabling a continuing response to the movements of God's grace.

Prayer and work

Uniting prayer with work, the occupation of the moment, enables work to become an expression of prayer. An early Christian writer wrote:

> The man who links together his prayer with deeds of duty and fits seemly actions with his prayer is the man who prays without ceasing. For his virtuous deeds or the command-ments he has fulfilled are taken up as part of his prayer. For only in this way can we take the saying 'praying without ceasing' as being possible, if we can say that the whole life of the Christian (saint) is one mighty integrated prayer. Of such prayer, part is what is usually called prayer and ought not to be performed less than three times a day.
>
> (St Isaac the Syrian)

In other words prayer as a specific activity is a normal part of the daily life of anyone who would be a friend of God. As such, it is the frame within which other activities, including work, can be legitimately regarded as in some sense real prayer. An important qualification is this. Our work and other activities must be the practical expression of the same attitude towards God that our prayer is also seeking to express. Take away the frame of prayer and the theory about work falls apart. Therefore, anyone who never or hardly ever prays, cannot claim his work to be part of his prayer. Instead, it becomes a substitute for prayer, and might even become a refusal to have anything directly to do with the *mystery* of God.

5

Approaching God

In the question of reading we should bear in mind the principal aim of our life and choose those things which accord with it. Then something will result that is integrated, coherent, and therefore strong. This solidity of knowledge and conviction will give strength also to our character as a whole.

Bishop Theophan

Spiritual reading

Spiritual reading is a way of approaching God that can kindle in us a sense of his presence and help us to become more aware of it. Let it become a prelude to prayer during which attention becomes gradually focused on God. One of the reasons for distraction in prayer could be that our hearts and minds are starved of this kind of nourishment. In this way of reading, the number of books read is not of primary importance, but the manner of the reading takes priority because it is more like meditation and prayer than the reading of a book in the ordinary sense. To be effective it needs to be punctuated by frequent pauses, so that on one level attention is being given to what the writer is saying, but on another level we look and listen to the effect that such reading is having deep within the heart. In the quietness and stillness of the heart ruminate on the passage being read and listen for the emotions being aroused, the inner echoes that are struck, and the subsequent aspirations towards God that spring up from the deep places of the heart.

Such slow and deliberate reading can lead the reader through the same experiences and aspirations that the writer is attempting to describe and articulate. The moment arrives when one moves from reading into the condition of an attentive listening to God, as one focuses one's attention on God's presence within.

Holy Scripture

Holy Scripture holds the primary place in spiritual reading. Those same wonderful works there described are now active and present through the sacraments, in the same God who acts and intervenes now. If what the Scriptures are about on the level of life comes alive in the prayerful Christian, that person will discover everything of which the Scriptures speak, not as mere words, but as the living reality of the present and active God. The public reading of the Scriptures in Eucharist and Office will become more immediately life-giving, as God breaks in upon our personal thought and prayer. In the spirit of St Augustine of Hippo we shall 'be alert and listen to the Gospel as though the Lord himself were present'.

Word and Sacrament become our manna from heaven, the heavenly manna fed into our hearts and minds by the reading and hearing of the Word of God, and fed into our bodies as we feed on the Bread of eternal life and drink the Cup of salvation. In the backyard of life we are fed on Word and Sacrament as we journey in the way of salvation as the New Israel of God's People. We will pass through the same saving experience as our ancestors of old to reach our fulfilment in and through Christ.

The experience may not always be one of joy and peace, light and joy, but may well bring the pain of the sword piercing to the bone and marrow, as the conscience is disturbed in the painful self-knowledge of wrong motives and actions. Allowing God to take us through the pain and the turmoil, darkness and death, empties us of what has been inhibiting our relationship with him and preventing our entry into the Promised Land of his life and love. The

Bible can never be a mere bedside book of uplifting comfort. Gregory the Great tells us that it is rather like a mirror in which we may see our inward face, and there come to know our ugliness and our beauty, realise what progress we are making and how far we are from improvement.

Ways of reading the Bible

There are several ways to read the Bible and people will find the way that best suits them. *The Bible Reading Fellowship Notes* is a good and helpful way that is reasonably cheap and issued three times a year. Explanatory notes explain the text of a reading for each day and the meaning or spirit of the passage is gathered into a prayer.

Another way is to read the Bible with the Church, alongside the sequence of the Christian Year that links Holy Scripture with the Church's doctrinal understanding of the Faith, as the great events of sacred history are commemorated in the Church's worship. Cycles of readings are provided in the *Book of Common Prayer* and in *Common Worship* for the Sunday Eucharist, with three lessons for each week. These lessons may be split up to provide daily Bible readings during the week preceding the Sunday. Some priests produce explanatory notes for the following Sunday readings, thus providing a valuable teaching aid, which not only assists the personal growth of their congregation, but also encourages a more intelligent participation in the Ministry of the Word in the Church's communal worship. Reading the Bible in this way provides it with a living context for worship, doctrine and life; the comprehensive perspective in which the true intention and total design of divine revelation can be detected and grasped. It also demonstrates that the sacraments are the expression of God in action.

Other systematic cycles of readings for Morning and Evening Prayer are provided. An ordered reading of a book from Old or New Testament might be read in a daily manner with the use of such tables of readings. Experimenting in these ways of reading the Bible might encourage the formation of a Bible-reading group to mutually assist each other in such ways of using and understanding the Bible.

Spiritual Classics

There are other sources of nourishment that can assist us towards maturity in the Christian life. These are called the spiritual classics because they have stood the passage of time and have sustained the lives of generations of Christians through the ages. There is so much of value in them for Christians down the ages, in the form of sound advice from masters of the spiritual life who have travelled the road before us, immersed in Word, Sacrament, and prayer. From their experience they have drawn maps to help others setting out on the same journey. Such books are too numerous to mention, and every book would not be of value to everyone, so that consultation with a wise priest or spiritual adviser is where help and guidance can be sought.

In *The Confessions* of St Augustine we find not a book of devotion but a work that enumerates clearly the principles of penitence, faith, and love, which are the permanent elements of all Christian devotion. Herein is the solemn address of a soul to God, recounting to the merciful God the penitent and grateful story of a life of many failures and repeated mercies, and so it speaks with power to every age. From a monastic writer in a fifteenth-century Europe of change and decay, but also a Europe of change and reconstruction that has similarities to our own in its social, economic, political, and religious instabilities, comes Thomas à Kempis's *The Imitation of Christ*. Like Mother Julian's *Revelations of Divine Love,* it illustrates an important point, that the greatest religious discoveries are made where the pressures are greatest. Julian of Norwich is described today as a woman of hope in the midst of death, despair, and destruction. This hope rests on something outside herself, on the Lord who is with us, 'our protector while we are here'. She has absorbed the essence of Scripture into her very being and distilled it into her life, so she can express it as a living wisdom for every age. The momentous changes since the fourteenth century have not blunted this wisdom, so that she is coming alive in our time because of our awareness of these same realities in her and in us, which transcend the passage of time. Christians of all denominations are identifying with her in their thirst for holiness, because she articulates it in a living way. They find in her an authentic witness to the life of prayer, which they seek. A classic from a post-Reformation Europe is Lorenzo Scupoli's *Spiritual Combat*, that is designed to give the necessary guidance and direction in the ways of spiritual growth in the active and busy life of the workaday world. Julian and Thomas à Kempis reveal the great principles of faith and vision which guide the soul on the upward path of union with God, while Scupoli deals with the actual difficulties of a soul surrounded with temptation and struggling with the deceitfulness of sin. Mention of some of these classics may be helpful. *The Devout Life,* quoted earlier, is by a French bishop of the seventeenth century, a great pastor and spiritual counsellor. He explains his purpose in a preface, 'My intention is to instruct those who live in towns, in families, and whose circumstances oblige them to lead to all intents and purposes an ordinary life.'

Historically for Anglicans, this type of devotional book goes back to 1576 when John Woolton published *The Christian Manuel/, or of the life and manners of true Christians.* His theme was to show 'how needefull it is for the servaunts of God to manifest and declare to the world: their faith by their deedes . . . and their profession by their conversation'. A hallmark of this devotion is that 'all justified men should walk *in a new obedience'*, and he encourages daily self-examination with prayer as an essential devotional discipline. Such devotion was grounded in doctrine, that can be noticed in the general and explicit theological presuppositions of the writers, and especially in passages concerning the Eucharist. So here in *The Christian Manuell* teaching on justification by faith is sensibly related to doing good works and the test of faith is seen to be the good life.

This kind of devotional book was meant to be an

elementary treatise of theology, with careful teaching on the nature of prayer, which would enable the reader to form his own petitions in his own words, with specimen devotions and meditations to guide him in doing so, together with directions for public and private duties. The basic premise was that everyone should have a clear understanding of religion, and laity should accept both spiritual and intellectual responsibility. The Anglican Reformation was, doctrinally, a return to the faith of the Early Church, and, in part at any rate, a return to the earlier type of devotion, where intellect is prior to Christian sentiment. The same effect was produced by a changed emphasis in the concept of liturgy itself. Anglicans stressed the principle of edification, which further strengthened the ascendancy of head over heart. Anglican piety rarely strayed very far from the spirit and fashion of the Liturgy; indeed it presupposes the *Book of Common Prayer* as a basis.

Bringing to the fore this principle of edification, combined with the calm and ordered piety of the Anglican liturgy, assisted the development of a more restrained and sober devotion in which there is a strong ethical tinge. The word 'reasonable' occurs frequently in connection with personal piety. The model is scriptural and influenced by the early Christian Fathers and is strongly ethical in the spirit of self-dedication. It is an exact and careful piety aiming at bringing all daily life under the lordship of Jesus Christ.

Unfortunately, not many Anglican devotional classics are in print, though they may be found in libraries or in a parish priest's study. *The Whole Duty of Man* was published anonymously in 1657, after the Civil War and on the Restoration of the Church of England. It dealt plainly with the moral duties of Christians and was inspired by the last words of the Book of Ecclesiastes, 'Fear God and keep the commandments: for this is the whole duty of man.' Here is a manual, probably the most influential of all, which became part and parcel of Anglican religious practice. It greatly helped the healing of the Church and the redirection of its energies, and by 1790 had reached twenty-eight editions. John Wesley used it and recommended it; confirmation candidates were given it for their future guidance and it was to be found in most homes and many churches. It continued as the standard book for the laity well on into the following century. Other Anglican classics of devotion include Jeremy Taylor's *Holy Living and Dying*, Robert Nelson's *Festivals and Fasts*, the poetry of George Herbert, Thomas Traherne and John Donne. From the seventeenth century comes *A Serious Call to a Devout and Holy Life* by the Anglican William Law, which had such an impact in renewing the Church and paving the way for the Evangelical Revival and The Oxford Movement that called the Church of England to holiness. Means and ends are always before the reader of these manuals. Scougal's *The Life of God in the Soul of Man* (1677) sees the end as 'a real participation in the Divine Nature' and the means is discipline, which opens our lives to faith and love, to humility and purity.

A book that comes out of the Russian Orthodox experience is autobiographical and has a personal interest. *The Way of a Pilgrim* (translated by R. M. French) is primarily about a man who wants to know and experience prayer at first hand. It illustrates how he draws his inspiration for prayer from the reading of the Bible and the *Philokalia*, a collection of sayings from spiritual masters in the Orthodox Tradition. These sayings are concerned with the interior life of contemplative stillness and union with God. There are numerous other publications currently in circulation about desert father devotion in collections of *Sayings of the Desert Fathers*, a useful edition being one by Thomas Merton. *The Art of Prayer, An Orthodox Anthology*, compiled by Igumen Chariton of Valamo, translated by Kadloubovsky and Palmer, is a collection of sayings on the essence and spirit of prayer and how to pray.

The point of such reading

The purpose of reading such books is not to fill the mind with facts, but to discover insights concerning oneself, the true self, and what changes are needed if spiritual growth is to bear fruit. At the same time, we are seeking a deeper knowledge and awareness of God and what it means to be a follower of Christ. Once these insights are given we must respond to them and let them affect us, allowing God to translate them into the different situations of our lives. The fact that Thomas à Kempis was a monk, Julian of Norwich an anchorite, and the pilgrim had a pattern of life peculiar to himself, does not imply our copying them in the way they lived. It is the spirit and principle of their discipleship that we must grasp. This was rooted in an ever-deepening awareness and knowledge of God that they communicate in a living way, and is of general application to all Christians. It is at that level of entering into a deeper knowledge and awareness of God that they help us, and from there we are to discover what this implies for our own lifestyle. The Introduction to *The Way of A Pilgrim* makes the point that readers must not 'ape' the pilgrim in any literal sense, but also draws attention to the fact that the pilgrim learned from a master much of the doctrine and teaching he appropriated into his own life. A wise spiritual guide and adviser are essential for anyone seeking a serious life of prayer.

Such writing speaks to the reader not merely as the transcript of a mere author, a storyteller, philosopher or even a friend. It speaks in some way, as one's own self. Therefore if what is read is listened to, things will be said that may not be written in these books. This will be due, not to those who have written them, but to the One who speaks in each one of us. Hence the appeal of such works to a wide and varied circle of readers, because they have touched the deepest springs of prayerful thought and personal devotion. We find in them a record of an actual experience that remains true to all time as a lasting testimony of human aspirations and needs.

What George Eliot wrote of Thomas à Kempis can in principle be applied to others who have given us a record of their experience. Eliot said:

> that even though he was a monk with a different pattern of life nevertheless, he was born of the same humanity, lived under the same silent far-off heavens with the same desires,

the same strivings, the same failures and the same weariness. The secret of the *Imitation's* charm lies in the fact that it is the faithful transcript of a soul, just an ordinary soul, gifted with no special endowments of intellect, favoured by no special opportunities of birth nor visited by any special fervours of ecstasy of spirit. Yet despite all the weary trials and perplexities of monastic life he was faithful in the following of Christ and was gladdened by fellowship with God.

To catch this spirit and principle of faithful discipleship can bring a new dimension of vitality and zeal into our own pilgrimage in the workaday world.

The threshold of prayer

Spiritual reading is a way of approaching God and can be invaluable in helping towards a more immediate awareness of God's presence, thereby stimulating the desire for God. It is the depth of our desire for God that gives reality to our prayer. The prayer of Julian of Norwich might well be made our own:

> God of your goodness give me yourself, for you are sufficient for me. I cannot properly ask anything less, to be worthy of you. If I were to ask *less,* I should always be in want. In you alone do I have all.
>
> (Julian's *Revelations,* ch. 5)

Our desire cannot be anything less than to be possessed by God, to discover, know and live with and in God, in the workaday world. Prayer is a means to that end. Having decided to pray that decision must be renewed each day so that we may continue to pray through all the changing scenes of life. Silence is the doorway to prayer, a stillness in which we wait that we may look and listen for signs of God's presence. Noises in memory, imagination and mind need to be stilled that we may hear the still small voice:

> Drop thy still dews of quietness
> Till all our strivings cease,
> Take from our souls the strain and stress
> And let our ordered lives confess the beauty of thy peace

Waiting and listening in such silence takes us from the surface of things into an experience of God as the first mover in prayer, ours, being a response to his loving initiative. Our own growth in prayer depends on our own willingness to listen that we may hear God speak. 'In the silence we learn to discern the voice of God from the other noises that voice their pleas in the whisperings of the subconscious self, the voices of the world, the clamour for personal ambition and vanity, the murmur of self-will and the fantasies of the imagination.'

Keeping the body still and relaxed will help one into such silence. So too will the restricting of one's vision, either by the closing of one's eyes or focusing them on something visual such as a crucifix or cross, an icon or picture, a lighted candle or flower. God is more than any of these symbols and so they are useless unless they point us beyond them to the personal reality that is infinitely greater than any of them.

God is a mystery not totally unknown. Fr Bryant writes:

> We know him as a child knows the ocean after a single visit to the seaside. He knows the look of the sea from the shore, he knows the feel of the water washing against his legs when paddling, and he knows the salt taste of the sea. But he doesn't know the ocean, its vast extent, its teeming life, and the contours of the ocean bed, its tides, its storms and its currents. So we know God and we don't know him. He abides a mystery altogether beyond our comprehension.

He goes on to tell us that mental pictures, symbols, truths expressed in words, can help us realise God's presence by evoking in us an awareness of what we might otherwise have ignored. They help to sharpen our perception of a Presence, there all the time, which we so easily fail to notice.

6

Words and Prayer

Enter into the spirit of the prayers which you hear and read, reproducing them in your heart; and in this way offer them up from your heart to God, as if they had been born in your own heart under the action of the grace of the Holy Spirit. Then, and then alone, is the prayer pleasing to God. How can we attain such prayer? Ponder carefully on the prayers which you have read in your prayer book; feel them deeply, even learn them by heart. And so when you pray you will express that which is already deeply felt in your heart.

Bishop Theophan

Words

Everyone uses words in which to express their prayer and finds that when they first begin to pray it is usually the only form of expression. As our prayer grows and deepens we begin to realise that there is more to it than an order of words. These are merely the expression of a deepening communion of heart and mind with God. Nevertheless, because words are the predominant medium of expression, this way of praying is called vocal. For many people it is their only way of praying, the words helping them to focus their attention on the ever present reality of God, and becoming the medium in which to express to him their thoughts and feelings, the adoration of their hearts and minds. They are tools of the mind, which enable us to express and so focus and direct thought and aspiration.

They lead into an awareness and experience of God and assist in holding attention to his presence. At the same time, they become the necessary and concrete way of expressing the affections of the heart and mind that God's presence stimulates within us.

A child beginning to talk first copies what other people say, and then repeats what it hears. Understanding grows when the child identifies the words with related objects and people. As vocabulary is acquired, the child begins to think and use these words to express what is in its heart and mind. Our capacity to pray grows in a similar kind of way. We use the words of other people, their prayers, at first thinking little about their meaning, until they begin to have a suggestive power that affect us as they move and modify the deeper levels of the soul. Using written prayers in this way, to express the sentiments of heart and mind, is a way into a deepening awareness of God. The words of the prayer do not need to be our own. Like the child, people need to be given words, so that they can gradually learn the language in which to express the thoughts and affections of heart and mind. Those prayers become the vehicle carrying us into an experience of a communion with God that they were first seeking to articulate.

For generations of Anglicans the *Book of Common Prayer* provided a language for their personal devotion. They learned to pray by joining in the Church's prayer and the Prayer Book became one of the most popular gifts at Confirmation. As a pastor one has a sympathy with those who felt bereft at the advent of the modern liturgies. Nevertheless, there is no reason why these forms of liturgical prayer should not become for the present generation a similar kind of stimulus to personal devotion. The *Alternative Service Book* (*ASB*) may not be legal for public worship, but there is no reason why people should not use it for private devotion. On page 97 there is a selection of *Prayers for Various Occasions* and on page 109 an *Index of Prayers*. Browsing through *Common Worship* may provide a selection of suitable prayers for personal use. From such a quarry of prayers, a selection can be taken and used to build one's own way of personal devotion. The more familiar the phrases of the Liturgy become, the more likely are they to be built into the language of one's own personal prayer placing it in a larger dimension. The weekly Collect can be used daily, along with prayers of praise and thanksgiving. The words of the General Confession and Absolution from the Eucharist can be used in a personal way. A useful aid would be the compiling of an anthology of such prayers in a book of personal devotion. Verses from the Psalms. Quotations from Scripture, and one's own prayers in brief sentences, can be woven into the pattern of such a book. It was such a practice that produced the classic manuals of private devotion of Lancelot Andrewes, William Laud, Thomas Wilson, and others of their era.

Personal and liturgical prayer can assist each other in this way. As the frequent and familiar use of such prayers becomes the marrow and backbone of one's personal prayer, they will nourish, affect, and form the soul at deep levels. The words of these prayers should be said slowly to allow them to draw the mind, heart, and body, into the prayer. Frequent repetitions can allow the words to awaken echoes within, for the prayer is more than an order of words and sometimes our interior aspirations are too deep for words. The words can then become a kind of windshield to prevent the aspirations being blown away, rather than an expression of an aspiration.

The need for a pattern

The words will need a certain pattern of thought, of attitude, that will guide the expressions of heart and mind. As there is a basic and well-trodden way of making an apple pie and the proof of it is in the eating, so too in prayer. There is a basic and well-trodden way that has given rise to four underlying attitudes, expressing itself in four acts of prayer. Many will testify that the proof of this way of praying lies in using it and allowing it to mould us into a pattern of prayer. The four parts of this pattern are familiar, *Adoration, Confession, Thanksgiving* and *Supplication*. The first letter of each word arranged in sequence makes up the word ACTS.

1. Adoration

Adoration means approaching God in an attitude of awe and wonder that one may delight in his beauty and majesty. To adore God is to recognise his completeness and uniqueness and oneself as limited and incomplete. Man has 'no rights' over God and has even forfeited the privileges bestowed upon him. The attitude of adoration openly acknowledges this and recognises that our Creator in his utter graciousness has not only revealed himself to us, but has come to give us life, abundant life in him.

Adoration has been described as telling God what you believe about him. 'Lord God, you made us, you know us, you love us; you are guarding us, guiding, helping, healing, warning', is a form of adoration. To prostrate the body, that is, to kneel resting the forehead on the floor, can deepen the act of adoration by involving the person more completely in it. I remember a Greek Orthodox priest telling me how his grandmother taught him to pray, by taking him along to the church and kneeling together in prayer, every few minutes she would place his forehead on the floor as they said the Jesus Prayer. Many a thoughtful Christian who believes in God with his head, but confesses that he never has any sense of God's presence, would begin to gain a realisation of God if he would prostrate himself and say slowly and with meaning the words of the Sanctus; or the verse from Psalm 95:11, *O come let us worship and fall down and kneel before the Lord our Maker: for he is the Lord our God and we are the people of his pasture and the sheep of his hand*. There are some who would say that to prostrate before God in this way is to treat him as some oriental tyrant, and it is degrading. Perhaps if we really thought of him as some oriental tyrant, then prostrating before him in this way would be true. But if we believe him to be a Mystery and Presence indwelling and sustaining us, a Mystery who has disclosed himself to us in Jesus Christ, then the more we exalt him the more we dethrone egoism, selfishness and pride, and the more we are set free to be our true selves and live our own truth. I believe that the act of prostration, like the act of kissing or embracing, is part of the age-old language of the body, and can express a meaning that cannot be wholly put into words.

Adoration is the most God-centred of the four acts and is the expression of a spirit of devotion in which we ask nothing for ourselves but express our praise and love. In marriage, the relationship grows and develops upon the necessity of each of the partners telling the other how wonderful they are in each other's eyes. The prayer of adoration is not a one-way traffic. God is active in opening up the way for richer and deeper experience, which stimulates thoughts and affections that find expression in *words*. The language of adoration may at first feel uncomfortable and alien to us. Words like 'bliss', 'beautiful', 'majesty', 'glorious', might initially jar our sensibilities. However, as experience increases and deepens, the prayer of Adoration uses fewer words and becomes more simple. In contemplation adoration becomes a simple gazing towards God.

2. Confession

Awareness of God is the fruit of adoration, which acts like a mirror that reflects a deeper self-knowledge. It is the same in human relationships. The truth about oneself is best refracted through what others can see. Standing alongside others can give one a glimpse of oneself if one is sufficiently sensitive and perceptive enough to see. When one sees other people possessing what one wants, success, good looks, cleverness, one may discover a jealous person lurking within. Failure to accept one's true self, oneself as one really is, more often than not spoils relationships. In consequence, a person's behaviour towards others is less likely to be motivated by love, 'the pure heart's desire', but by the worst kind of human covetousness. Patience is a virtue that many people claim to possess, until an awkward neighbour moves in next door. When such a moment of truth is acceptable, the relationship becomes the place where such patience can become real. The awkwardness might be a relative thing in the neighbour, in that the neighbour is only awkward to the extent that he meets awkwardness in others. Relation-

ship with God or with other people can be the place of
self-discovery, the mirror in which is reflected an image of
my real and true self, the kind of person I really am. A
person possesses three selves; the one he thinks he is, the
one other people think he is, and the one he really is. In
adoration the truth about oneself begins to dawn, the
Light shows up where things have been going wrong. It
may be in the way one has been missing the mark in the
evasion of duty, or facing for the first time some piece of
dishonesty, the hurtful or selfish word to someone, the
failure to honour the keeping of promises. Responsibility
and blame for such failures is put firmly in the right place,
on oneself. Then with God's help one strengthens one's
purpose to try and avoid such failures in the future.

There is also a need to acknowledge within oneself the
bad inclinations, particular dislikes and fears which it
seems impossible to prevent. These find expression in bad
moods and undue anxieties, depression, listlessness,
resentments and irritations. Often there is a clinging to
these habitual responses to life and a despairing that they
can never be broken. Think of the habitual communicant
receiving the Sacrament but who is always careful not to
kneel next to the person to whom he or she will not speak
or pass the peace. Watching television soaps can be infor-
mative in showing us stereotyped and habitual behaviour
traits, the root cause of which stems from centering one's
life round one's own interests and not around God and
neighbour. Acknowledgement that such flaws in oneself
inhibit our relationship with God is absolutely necessary.
It is to be done, not in a spirit of self-reproach but in a
spirit that is seeking healing and deliverance. It is difficult
to draw a line between the evil that is one's own responsibility and for which one must be blamed, and the evil
from which one must be delivered. The distinction is
important when it comes to accepting responsibility for
wrongdoing and apportioning blame. Accepting blame for
what one can help strengthens one's will to do better, but
blaming oneself for something which is not one's own
fault, and therefore which one cannot help, leads to
despair.

To come to God in a spirit of repentance is to come

seeking a complete and radical renewal of one's emotional and mental attitude. It does not merely mean an acknowledgement and contrition for sins but more precisely a 'change of mind'. The hope that God holds out to us is the power of the Gospel to do just this that he might share his life with us.

3. *Thanksgiving*

Being thankful does not always come naturally or spontaneously. We are inclined to take so much in life for granted until it seems that things are not going in the way we had anticipated. Human friendship is not something we limit to times of need such as the sharing of sympathy or when a problem occurs. True friendship shares the joys as well as the sorrows of life, the mundane and the trivial. Friendship with God should reflect itself in the same kind of way. Yet often he is only sought in times of trouble, and because there seems to be no other kind of help available. It is easy to slip into an attitude of mind that never thinks of God when everything in the garden is lovely. Yet times of gladness and joy should lead naturally into thankfulness to God for making life so sweet, finding a natural place in our prayer for the kind of thank you that is a spontaneous response.

A simple starting point into a spirit of thankfulness is a backward glance over the day's events. In some of the simplest and basic necessities of life there will be much for which to be thankful. Simple experiences of kindness and love, friendships and joys that have been shared, these are some of the things it is so easy to take for granted and allow to pass without a nodding thank you. Self-pity that gives rise to a depressive moaning about life stems from a forgetfulness of such blessings. An ever-deepening spirit of thankfulness in our lives will give birth to a more compassionate prayer for those who are less fortunate.

There is something much more fundamental in Christian thanksgiving. It is a spirit that Our Lord compared to the attitude of the 'birds of the air' and the 'lilies of the field'. It is the need for absolute trust and confidence in God's love for each one of us. God loves his children and gives us all we need, even his only Son. Do not be anxious then and do not be afraid is Our Lord's advice. Being thankful to God inevitably leads to a deep trust that God will provide all we need. Thankfulness is the antidote to depression and anxiety.

The Cross and Resurrection has transformed everything so that whatever comes in life, even suffering itself, can become something for which to thank God. Sifting one's experience in the light of this perspective not only widens one's vision of the things for which to be thankful, but helps us to discern things for which at first sight it may have been difficult to be thankful, and which in the end turned out to be a blessing. In this way the spirit of gratitude grows and enables us to see potential for enrichment in all the events of daily experience. 'Counting our blessings' ceases to restrict it to the good things that happen to us, the things we evaluate as good. It enables us to include within that orbit some of the difficult and painful experiences. Keeping a place for such regular expressions of thankfulness will open the eyes to see God in his work of love in our daily lives. Soon there will emerge unsuspected occasions to thank him constantly.

4. Supplication

Supplication means quite simply the prayer of asking, and has two categories. The first is Intercession, which is primarily praying for others, and the second is Petition in which one prays for oneself. St Thomas Aquinas gave two good reasons for this kind of prayer. First, it enables us to cooperate with God's providence, and secondly, through such prayer our confidence in God is awakened. Supplication is not attempting to persuade God to change his mind or to bring him round to our way of thinking. Its primary aim and purpose is co-operation with God in bringing about his will. There are some things which God wills, but will not bring about uninvited and unasked. God knocks at the door of our lives, he does not force his way in. In petition, we open a door for God to enter, so that he can bring about his will in ways that we cannot predict.

As we grow in a confident reliance on God, so there

grows between him and us a deepening relationship, as of a child living in and enjoying the security of a father. Our prayer for others emerges from our sense of this nearness of God. Like us, they are under the eyes of God's love, and because of this they are under the eyes of our love too. Only in so far as we are in tune with this love can we love to any effect. When we think of them at this place of nearness to God, it is through the presence of God with them and with us, that our love in complete co-operation with God's love for both of us is brought to effectiveness in their lives. In this way we lift to God the thoughts and desires of our hearts, that they may be placed within the total and all-embracing perspective of God's will and purpose. There they find their harmony or discord, and if need be, are adjusted to the tune of the divine will.

By so doing we will discover that God always does answer prayer, though it may not be in the form of our own anticipations and it might take much longer than we have been prepared to allow. St Monica, the mother of St Augustine of Hippo, prayed for ten years for the conversion of her son before it actually happened. Perseverance in prayer is therefore necessary because of the barricades of distrust that may have to be broken down, not only in those for whom we pray, but also in those of us who are praying, before God can act.

The prayer of Supplication helps us to share confidently in God's concern for the whole of his creation. It helps us to see and know the detail and the particulars of this concern, as it gives us an insight into the many barricades that are erected to keep God out. This enables us to persist in the spirit of that carefree confidence seen in the 'birds of the air' and the 'lilies of the field'. Only in so far as we let go of the barricades of anxiety and mistrust in ourselves can we become the God-bearers, in whom those for whom we pray will find the Light and Life, which brings hope and strength, healing and salvation.

7

Intercession

When our spirit is fervent within us we are wont to pour forth for others also, making intercession either for those who are dear to us, or for the peace of the whole world.

John Cassian

The closeness of God

Everyone lives within the immediate presence of God yet for many people this nearness of God is unacknowledged, though he is equally present to all people. Nevertheless, some are more aware of it, and the closer one comes to God the more that awareness increases. This growing awareness of God is what brings us into the heart of prayer. As our vision of God widens so too does our prayer, as it seeks to be identified with the interests and concerns of God and become less concerned with self. Perspectives are unconsciously altered and these cause remarkable changes within. As prayer becomes less concerned with self and more concerned with God, it becomes more interested in the real needs of other people. There grows a new awareness of people as their needs occupy more and more of our prayer, in our own awakened sense of God's compassionate love for them, and this enables us to enfold them in our prayer. Our own harmony with such love makes our own loving effective, and prayer for others a necessary part of our lives, as God who is present to both of us, brings his love to bear on those for whom we pray.

God's response to our prayer

God does not 'jump in' miraculously to satisfy the requests of our prayer. He works in a more subtle way. Certain regularities of law are built into the very structure of human life that are necessary for our growth in freedom, understanding, and love. Within this structure, where we also experience inhibiting factors attempting to frustrate God's intention for human life, there is a potential for fulfilment. His influence begins to work when the 'natural' endowments of the spirit are opened to the transforming love of God. Bishop John Baker explains it like this:

> If natural telepathy for example, can communicate ideas and feelings across half a world, as well as attested cases suggest, then there is something, as yet imperfectly understood by us, some capacity of Man, to be open to non-physical reality. Prayer is not telepathy; but at the natural level it may use this openness. For if our weak human affections can link up through seemingly impassable obstacles and separations, why should not the power of God's love, which at all times is immediately present to each of us, penetrates the self, brings strength, joy, healing, and fortitude, prompting to this or that action? When we and those for whom we pray are bound in the deepest possible personal union by the common reality of God, when our love for them and theirs for us are consciously in tune and harmony with his will for us all, is it in any way incredible that the work of love should be done? That prayer, in short, should be 'answered'.[1]

The Bishop goes on to admit that this may be a groping in words after something half-glimpsed, half-guessed at; but it does chime in with what we know of the natural order, 'albeit on the outer frontier of the small province of that order as yet known to us'. The harmony of such a way of thinking with our understanding of God enables us to think along such general lines when trying to comprehend the efficacy of such prayer. 'It is the openness of the human self to the power of the divine love mediated through the activity of prayer, that we may most reasonably attribute those

[1] *The Foolishness of God*, London, DLT, 1970, p. 384.

cases of healing, guidance and inspiration, for many of which the evidence is so strong.'

We must be prepared to accept that God will work within earth's conditions, which includes holy words and sacraments. These are the media God uses, and through these instruments he will order human life in the same way that he has done with other instruments with which he has ordered what is for our good. A simple example is the family, to provide us with what is needful for our birth and growth. God has established certain conditions of life that are necessary if we are to grow and develop humanly.

In the universe there is a twofold and interlocked order the natural and the human. In the first, the order is 'relatively fixed', in the second, it is 'relatively flexible'. There is a world of regularities and a world of freedoms, both of God's making, and together they constitute the conditions in relation to which we must normally expect him to act in our regard. If the favourable answer to our petition requires a disruption of these regularities, like the miraculous mending of the damaged capsule bringing the astronauts to earth, one sees no evidence that the petition is answerable. One cannot say that the Tower of Siloam of which Our Lord speaks, fell and killed eighteen men in spite of prayers; but Our Lord seems to allude to the accident as if the spiritual attitudes of the victims had no bearing on the situation.

So in the natural order the regularities can bring bane or blessing because hazard is part and parcel of God's creation. Nevertheless, whatever happens to us in the created order does not fall outside God's caring concern, nor does the bane or the hazard ever suggest that God does not value us. Life is not all sunshine and rain is needed to make certain kinds of fruit to grow. The sun shines and the rain falls on the just as well as on the unjust. Saints as well as sinners find not only a share in the world's joy; they can also be victims of the world's tragedy and suffering. The same is true in the realm of human freedom; God's love is consistently active. He will not compel in a way that overrides human freedom, even when our prayer harmonises with what he wants. Even when the Spirit of God attempts to quicken and attract, having done so, he waits for a free response because he respects human freedom. It is this freedom that constitutes our humanity, and his respect for it demonstrates the true nature of love, which must always be free from compulsion. He works with the nature he has created, and in bringing a desire to good effect he allows the regularities and flexibilities into which the petition is released, a part in the operation. So the outcome of petitionary prayer is contingent on the conditions attending it. To illustrate this, think of many petitions that must be made by students before important examinations. Such prayer is fruitless unless there is something in the mind of the student on which the Spirit of God can work. The extent to which God can help will be dependent upon the student's co-operation before the examination, in his willingness to prepare his mind with the resources of hard study.

For every task determinative conditions are either present or lacking. What can be done, we must ask, within such conditions? As a petition is laid before God he also may consider ways and means for dealing with the goodness in the desire. If law is a necessity of the created order to secure to us serviceable constancies, and our petition involves overriding one such irregularity, then so far as we can see he does not have this solution to work with. At least he does not provably work with it in uncountable situations. Again, if what we ask involves compelling somebody's will, then so far as we can see he does not have this solution to work with. He does not visibly exercise compulsion over human freedoms. Again, if what we ask would involve us in some attitude or action which we could not and should not take, he does not have this solution to work with; and however unwilling we may be to admit some personal inadequacies or ignorance, they may be quite real.

What can we expect?

The spirit of Our Lord in Gethsemane is the spirit in which we must bring our petitions before God. To bring the

Gethsemane spirit, 'If it be possible ... the thine not mine' with our petitions, is to acknowledge that there might be factors at work of which we are ignorant and these can assist or prevent God from bringing our desire to good effect. This spirit helps to open up in us the conditions necessary for God to effect a change in us as we become more interested in his concerns, and this is the fruit of a deepening awareness of what the prayer of intercession involves. His love begins to transform us in such a way that the unchangeable element in the situation for which prayer is being offered can be accepted. There begins to grow a realistic trustful reliance on God's willingness to answer our prayer in the way that is open to him, as we cease to expect an answer that will measure up to our own prescribed blueprint. It is this humbler faith and trust that sustains us not only when the sun is shining but during those times when there is nothing but rain. This spirit is at the heart of the Lord's Prayer, 'Thy will be done, on earth as it is in heaven.' It does not preclude our own wishes and doubts, as Our Lord demonstrated in Gethsemane, for they are the very form that our prayer must take.

> Our intercession must always express itself in personal and specific terms. Are these terms there just to be overruled or ignored when they do not coincide with God's wiser knowledge of what is best? Such thinking reduces our prayer into an external and impersonal conception. Our particular requests spring from the common life we share with those for whom we pray, and become the concrete articulation at the conscious level of the unseen but real bond that unites us. Because that bond is a living one of mutual influence, they do not merely state the possibilities to which we suppose the other person might be open. They help to create openness for these things. When, therefore, through this natural medium of our psychical communion the love of God is brought to bear on the other person, its power works within the existing potentials, and thus issues in those very changes (or ones akin to them) for which we have asked. In this way human freedom is respected, human cooperation with God is made real and yet prayer is genuinely answered, and because the relationship is truly personal throughout there are no automatic fulfilments. There may be obstacles that even the love of God cannot yet overcome. But equally there is no

reason to doubt that if, as happens especially often when the human relationship is close and deep and alive with the genuine spirit of Christ, what is prayed for happens, then the prayer has indeed helped to bring about what people by themselves could never have done and what even God could not have done without our aid. This is not blasphemy. If we think of the great human destinies of freedom, understanding, and love, God has designed, and which he will always respect, then it is not incredible but probable. Furthermore, that living communion at the unconscious level that all people undoubtedly enjoy, even though contemporary individualistic western man has forgotten it, is now seen to have not merely a natural but a supernatural purpose. Like so many other aspects of the created order it proves to have a special relevance not only to this age, but also to the Age to come. It has its part to play in the kingdom.[2]

Praying for the dead

Central to the Christian life is the life and death of Christ, lived out in a person in which the human and the divine were perfectly balanced, so that while it is situated in space and in time it is not limited by these things in the way in which our lives are limited. This person came and 'dwelt among us' in a particular place and time, within an historic moment. It came to be described as a time of new creation, because the limitations of death were broken down to affect all human history before and after. God comes to live in the human and the human is taken to live in the divine. Jesus makes it possible for us to live with him in the life he lives with the Father in the Holy Spirit so that the things of God become the things of man. This is what makes us realise that for which we are made; Augustine's restlessness and longing which never goes away until we find our rest in God. We become truly human when we share fully in the very life and nature of God.

This is what the Creed describes as 'the communion of saints', meaning the reality of a communion of life in which the Christian lives with God, sharing the very life he

1. Baker, *The Foolishness of God*, pp. 387–8.

lives with his Son in the Holy Spirit. The sacraments enable us to share in God's life, to live in the eternal in the midst of human life, to experience here and now life in God's Kingdom. To live in this reality is to discover that the very things that would destroy our humanity are themselves overcome and defeated in the presence of him who is the God not of the dead but of the living.

The experience of the 'not yet in the now' becomes particularly evident when the Christian nears death. Baptism conformed our lives to the death and resurrection of Christ, through the coming of the Spirit (we die with him that we may be raised with him). The life of discipleship is where this is worked out in the joys and sorrows of faith, prayer, obedience and love in action in the workaday world. Those of us who have ministered to the dying can see this blossoming at such moments.

When Nicholas Ferrar, a seventeenth-century Cambridge scholar and man of prayer, was dying, he called the family and other friends together and asked them to say the prayers for a dying man. His biographer tells us that he seemed to fall into a peaceful sleep for a time, but they remained with him in the room. 'Suddenly he raised himself up in bed. His voice became clear and strong and, stretching out his arms, he looked upward and around him with a light of great happiness in his eyes. "O what a blessed change is here!" he cried ... "What do I see? ... I have been at a great feast. O magnify the Lord with me." One of his nieces spoke to him. "At a great feast dear father?" "Aye", he answered, "at a great feast, the great King's feast." They waited in expectation for him to continue but instead he laid back quietly on his bed, closed his eyes and lips and gave a long gasp.'[3] It was one o'clock when his soul departed, the time at which for years past he had always risen for his morning prayers. The awareness of the presence of God in which he had prayerfully lived and by means of which he had shared in the things of eternity in the midst of human life, he begins to glimpse more fully in the joy of the Father's Presence he is being invited to enter. In such situations we can only

[3.] A. L. Maycock, *Nicholas Ferrar*, London, SPCK, 1938, p. 299.

stand and watch a person experiencing what is at that present moment beyond our reach.

> Saints departed even thus
> Hold communion still with us;
> Still with us beyond the veil
> Praising, pleading, without fail.

> For
> ... in, Sacrament and prayer
> Each with other hath a share;
> Hath a share in tear and sigh,
> Watch and fast and litany.

This hymn is affirming what in every Eucharist we always affirm; it is always 'with angels and archangels and all the company of heaven', that our worship is united in a living and real way. The world of time and the world of eternity is a continuum of life and not disconnected compartments of reality. They interpenetrate and affect each other in the unceasing prayer of those who find their love for each other centred in God. In such prayer we discover that the 'communion of saints' is a family in which the stronger help the weaker, a family in which we may all pray to one another and all pray for one another, a family created by the birth of the God-Man through the Holy Spirit, and the response of blessed Mary. Such an understanding of the communion of saints helps us to grasp the insight of the Russian theologian Alexei Khomyakov and to see the Church as saints participating with saints. His lines about his children help us to grasp what we understand ourselves to be doing when we pray for those who have died. His children had died and this is what he wrote:

> Time was when I loved still at midnight to come,
> My children, to see you asleep in your room;
> The Cross's holy sign on your foreheads to trace,
> And commend you in prayer to the love and the grace
> Of our gracious and merciful God.

> Dear children at that same still midnight do ye,
> As I once prayed for you, now in turn pray for me;
> Me who loved the Cross on your foreheads to trace;
> Now commend me in turn to the mercy and grace
> Of our gracious and merciful God.

We pray for the departed because we love them in the love which comes from God, and believing them to be nearer God than we are, we are sure that they pray for us more strongly within that same love. Even though after the Reformation prayers for the dead came to be forbidden, the practice re-emerges in our tradition because it seems natural and right. The seventeenth-century Anglican divine and Bishop of Edinburgh, William Forbes, assures us when he writes,

> The Fathers, certainly, 'being led', (to use the words of Cassandar) 'by the testimonies and examples of Scripture, from which it is evident that the prayers which just men offer for others are of great avail with God; and being moreover certainly persuaded that the righteous at their death do not cease to be, but, joined to Christ, lead a blessed life', and that they pray for us now much more ardently than ever before, inasmuch as they are endued with a greater love than formerly, and (as S. Cyprian says) 'are secure of their own immortality and anxious for our safety' – the Fathers, I say, desired very greatly that during their pilgrimage in this life they might be aided by the prayers of those who were reigning in heaven (a thing which no one will say not to be lawful) and even asked it, so far, namely, as the saints have a knowledge of our condition. For although it be altogether uncertain whether they have an *idiopatheia* (to use the expression of some Protestants,) that is, a particular acquaintance with our necessities and distresses, yet, who in his senses would deny to them a sympathy *(sumpatheia)* or general knowledge, derived from the word of God and the recollection of their own past experience? And the Fathers declared this their wish and desire, by calling upon them, either all in general, or even some particular individuals of them by name, both in their public and in their private prayers, as being present in spirit and soul; not to constitute them propitiatory mediators with God in the highest sense: but that by their prayers (which they believed to be of great avail with God) joined also to their own prayers, they might more easily obtain their

desires from God the Father through the only Mediator and Propitiator, Christ.[4]

Prayer for the departed is not concerned to ask God to shower the departed with heavenly benefits. Look at it like this:

> God has made and sustains that which we are; and that includes the continuum of our human relationships. Why should we suppose that he who upholds us through and beyond death will denature us by stripping out this essential part of our being? ... And if this continuum is there, why should we imagine that God's love and truth will not still make use of it, as they did before, to find their way into the heart of those for whom we pray, judging, purifying, transforming by joining forces with our love for them, coming in its company, being welcomed on its surety? So long as the personal identity exists, and stands in the presence of God. Prayer makes sense; and death sets the person praying and the one, prayed no farther apart than they were in this life.[5]

Khomyakov's lines make plain that help should come in the reverse direction, that those who have died should in their turn help us by their prayers. Surely the more their capacity for love is purified and deepened by God's love and truth, the more effective we could expect their cooperation with God to be on our behalf. Again it is not for our profit that we ask them to pray but that 'their prayer for us and their joint-prayer with us are always active to make us more alive and open to the reality of God, and more at home where we should be most at home – with them and him.'[6] That is where as Christians we live, in that family, the 'communion of saints', a family in which we may all pray to one another and all pray for one another. Wherever this doctrine is neglected it gives rise to an unhealthy preoccupation with 'getting in touch with the dead', the *raison d'être* of spiritualism, which is not the same thing.

---

4. William Forbes, 'Concerning the Invocation of Angels and Saints', *Considerationes Modestae*, (Library of Anglo-Catholic Theology), Oxford, J. H. Parker, 1856, vol. II, ch. 3, p. 231.
5. Baker, *The Foolishness of God*, pp. 389–90.
6. Ibid., p. 391.

Costly but necessary

Intercession is costly but necessary work, an important
and vital part of a Christian's prayer. It will demand time,
care and energy and a readiness to apply all these to
people who may not only be strangers but enemies. What
better starting point to the loving of our enemies? Faithfulness is what will be required. Personal intercession will
find its significance in the fact that it is a loving part of the
intercession of the whole Body of Christ. It is impossible
to identify the needs of those for whom we pray because
our understanding of them is limited and we might well
get it all wrong. God knows perfectly well the real needs
of those for whom we pray. All that is necessary is to hold
up to God the people for whom we pray and places for
which we pray. Leave them with him and pass on.

Petition

In praying for oneself the spirit of such prayer cannot be a
selfish preoccupation with what 'I think I need'. Such
prayer is about our own involvement with God in the situation of life as it is, that is, in our own backyard in the
workaday world. This will take account of life not only in
relationship with God but also in other relationships and
will bring into such prayer the loves, hopes, fears and
responsibilities of such relationships. Our praying will aim
at deepening our general insight into the very character
and values of God and the situation of human life as it is.
As we sit before the television set and watch drama, news,
soaps, documentaries, listen to the radio and the influence of all the activities of life in which we have to be
involved, we must watch, see and understand. All this can
inform us of what is happening in God's world and
discern something of his presence that we might know
and understand more of God and the human condition.
All this can stir new responses of the heart which can
enliven our own personal prayer of petition as we seek
true understanding of our Christian discipleship within
this larger scene of human life as a partner of God.

8

Thinking and Praying

Unless our mental prayer does something to awaken in us a consciousness of our union with God, of our complete dependence on Him for all our vital acts, in the spiritual life, and of His constant loving presence in the depths of our souls, it has not achieved the full effect for which it was intended.

Thomas Merton

Speaking to God, slowly and reflectively in words, is the way in which most people find their way into prayer. For some it is a medium of prayer that lasts them a lifetime, the staple diet that leads them into a deepening communion with God. While words should always continue to be part of everyone's prayer, for some there comes a time when it becomes less and less satisfying as the staple diet of their prayer and gives rise to feelings of frustration. The temptation is to press on in the same old way or give up altogether. This will happen if such feelings of frustration are not seen as a moment of significance; the signalling of a time of growth in prayer rather than of disintegration. Such a perception helps one to see the need to change one's way of praying.

Meditation

What is happening is a growing desire to be less concerned with the words of prayer and a need to be more

concerned with the thoughts the words have been stimulating within. It is a desire to be more concerned with
thinking about God, reflecting upon ideas and thoughts
born from one's increasing knowledge of God. The word
'meditation' is used to describe this way of praying
because it literally means the pursuing of a line of
thought. Archbishop Anthony Bloom would say that in
meditation one is 'pursuing a piece of straight thinking
under God's guidance' where the aim is to assimilate and
appropriate what is being suggested about God in the
'piece of straight thinking'. The rational or thinking power
of the soul has the upper hand initially in this way of
praying but it cannot continue like that. What is suggested
to the mind about God must be allowed to engage the
feelings of the heart and lead a person into a living experience of God. The thinking has initially stimulated our
desire for God, but our thoughts cannot remain in the
head, directing and governing everything in the soul. The
thoughts must be allowed to descend into the heart so
that the heart can feel what the mind is thinking and
thereby take the initiative in prayer.

An illustration will help. It is often said that absence
makes the heart grow fonder. Think of a couple who love
each other, and then find themselves in different places at
a particular moment in their lives. The husband thinks of
his wife and allows his mind to picture what she might be
doing. These thoughts and imaginative pictures of her
cannot remain the cold concern of reason but inevitably
stir in his heart the feelings of love he has for her, as he
ponders their past life together and looks forward to a
time of interrupted bliss when they are reunited. Change
the subject of this man's thoughts replacing his wife with
God and there is an illustration of what is meant by meditation. God is the one we love and of whom we think. Our
thoughts turn to consider what he has said and done in
revealing himself and then naturally go on to reflect what
he is like, anticipating the time when we shall enjoy him
forever in uninterrupted communion and life. These
thoughts in the mind stir in our hearts the feelings of love
that motivate a desire for union with him.

This way of prayer is also called mental prayer because

the main preoccupation is to think and ponder certain truths to keep the mind from wandering. Such prayer cannot be the exclusive activity of the head alone but must involve the heart in affection and love. There can be no dissociation from the mind that knows God and the heart that loves him. Meditation must involve thinking and loving, the head and the heart united, because it is only through love that we can identify with God that we might live in him and experience the Truth as love. Hence meditation must always be a personal participation and sharing in the life of God who is Truth and not a mere piece of detached and objective thinking about him. Only by involving affections and thoughts can this happen.

Meditation then is more than a practical intellectual exercise or even the attempt to impress upon our minds the mystery of the Christian Faith. The time of meditation is not a time of study on the devotional level because we do not seek to know God as if he were an object over us like other objects. We seek to know him in himself that we may be possessed by the Truth, not by mere thinking but also by loving. Alongside the thinking must go the consecration of the spirit, what is going on in the heart, which of necessity involves the will. It is love that intensifies and clarifies our thinking and gives it an affective element. Through love the heart is stirred to take off into prayer and enabled to appreciate the value hidden in the supreme truth that our thinking has begun to seek and to which it has been leading. This affective element transforms our meditation from cold reasoning into loving prayer, into a dialogue in being where we wait in adoration to experience the transfiguring and converting power of God's presence.

Thomas Merton describes mental prayer as a kind of 'sky-rocket'. A spark of divine love kindles the soul and moves it heavenward as we think about God.

> Mental prayer is therefore something like a sky-rocket. Kindled by a spark of divine love. The soul streaks heavenward in an act of intelligence as clear and direct as the rocket's trail of fire. Grace has released all the deepest energies of our spirit and assists us to climb to new and unsuspected heights. Nevertheless our own faculties soon reach

their limit. The intelligence can climb no higher into the sky. There is a point where the mind bows down its fiery trajectory as if to acknowledge its limitations and proclaim the infinite supremacy of the unattainable God.

But it is here that our 'meditation' reaches its climax. Love again takes the initiative and the rocket 'explodes' in a burst of sacrificial praise. Thus love flings out a hundred burning stars, acts of all kinds, expressing everything that is best in man's spirit, and the soul spends itself in drifting fires that glorify the Name of God while they fall earthward and fall away in the night wind.[1]

Merton goes on to quote St Albert the Great in his contrasting of the contemplation of the philosopher and the contemplation of the saints:

The contemplation of the philosophers seeks nothing but the perfection of the one contemplating and it goes no further than the intellect. But the contemplation of the saints is fired by the love of the one contemplated, that is, God. Therefore it does not terminate in an act of the intelligence but passes over into the will by love.

The contemplation of the philosophers, which is merely intellectual speculation on the divine nature as it is reflected in creatures, would be like a sky-rocket that soared into the sky but never went off. The beauty of the rocket is in its 'death' and the beauty of mental prayer and of mystical contemplation is in the soul's abandonment and total surrender of itself in an outburst of praise in which it spends itself entirely to bear witness to the transcendent goodness of the infinite God. The rest is silence.

Let us never forget that the fruitful silence in which words lose their power and concepts escape our grasp is perhaps the perfection of meditation. We need not fear and become restless when we are no longer able, 'to make acts'. Rather should we rejoice and rest in the luminous darkness of faith. This 'resting' is a higher way of prayer.

[1] Thomas Merton, *Spiritual Direction and Meditation and What is Contemplation?*, Wheathamstead, Anthony Clarke, 1975, pp. 45–6.

The way of meditation

Meditation is concerned with some aspect of God's self-revelation and so the Scriptures become our primary source. The text of the Bible can be read reflectively and slowly. Some of the Sunday readings from the *ASB* or *Common Worship* or *Book of Common Prayer* or passages suggested for daily reading in Bible-reading notes, can form the subject matter for one's meditation. Using the Church's liturgical readings not only links it up with liturgical prayer but also makes the important connection between doctrine and worship. The fruit of such meditation can be an important informing element that is fed into weekly worship. Other source material might be the daily New Testament readings for Morning or Evening Prayer. They can provide a systematic way of meditatively pondering the Scriptures and once again relate one's meditation to the great doctrinal themes of the Christian Year.

Another source of useful material can be found in the parables or miracle stories, the birth narratives or passion narratives. In St John's Gospel there are the 'I am' sayings; 'I am the Good Shepherd', 'I am the Light of the world', 'I am the vine you are the branches'. The New Testament epistles provide material for meditation upon some of the great doctrinal themes of our faith, the fruit of St Paul's deep meditation and personal apprehension of God. Commentaries and books based on the Bible will give help with new insights and new approaches to familiar passages.

The Psalms are another way of quietly thinking about God. They plumb the heights and depths of man's experience of God and if we are prepared to let the psalmist carry us into a sharing of that experience, our prayer will find inspiration, more especially when it chimes in with what has been happening in ourselves.

Finally, let us not forget the spiritual classics. As they chart the pilgrimage of the human soul in its journey towards union with God, what is written can strike chords that harmonise with our own experience. As such they can be the starting point for our own meditation.

Ways of meditation

There are many ways which might be listed, but that would be more confusing than helpful. Three ways are suggested and may well be the starting point for a person to find their own.

1. St Francis de Sales

His *Introduction to the Devout life* has been mentioned. In Book II he devotes the first nine chapters to prayer and meditation. By way of preparation, four possible ways of placing oneself in the presence of God are suggested.

Preparation
(i)   *Remember* God is everywhere and therefore he is here now.
(ii) *Remember* that He is in the depths of our own being and therefore very close to us.
(iii) *Reflect* that Our Lord and all the saints look upon us here and now.
(iv) *Use* the imagination to make these undoubted truths more vivid.

Then ask God's help to make the meditation

Composition of place

Having decided beforehand what the subject of medita-tion is to be, use the imagination and attempt to picture it as if it were a real event occurring in the present. Be careful to confine the attention to the subject of the medi-tation so that it may not roam all over the place.

Reflection

Take one or more considerations in order. Let these stim-ulate our love for God and divine things. This is what differentiates meditation from study. Our thoughts and reflections are made with a view to acquiring virtues and the love of God. The meditation must be a gentle and simple responsiveness to the subject that leads on quite naturally to movements of the will and affections.

Resolution

It is important not to let these desires remain a kind of empty delight, but resolve to bring them down to something quite concrete in one's own life.

Thanksgiving

Conclude with a thanksgiving for graces received and a restrained return to the ordinary occupations of life, but in such a way that the thoughts and attitudes produced by the meditation may not be too quickly or easily dispersed again.

Two Simple Methods

First Method

1. Prepare

Take time and do not rush because that is what kills prayer. The subject for meditation may have been forming for some time before actually settling down to pray. Spiritual reading helps and may suggest a subject for the following night's meditation. This is called remote preparation.

A more immediate preparation seeks a particular time, place, silence and stillness in which to place oneself at the disposal of the Holy Spirit, calling to mind the presence of God. The hymn 'Come Holy Ghost our souls inspire' can be used.

2. Picture

Read the passage slowly, bringing the imagination into play by trying to visualise the scene. Spend four or five minutes quietly re-reading in a slow and deliberate way, pausing where necessary.

3. Ponder

Allow the mind to think about the meaning of what is read. Ask questions. What did it mean then? What does it mean now? What ought I to do about it? Have a notebook and pencil to jot down any thoughts.

Talk to God directly about what your pondering suggests and let this prayer lead you into thanksgiving, penitence, adoration or intercession as seems appropriate. The meditation should be rather like a mirror in which to see something of oneself and where and how one needs to grow.

4. Promise

Bring it down to something positive and definite. Beware of impractical and insincere resolutions. Let them be small and practical and something that can be done fairly soon during the same day. It may be a resolution to be more alert and take note how the fruit of meditation can be related to one's life during the day.

Second Method

This allows more use of the imagination.

1. Preparation

Again it can be remote or immediate. Reading the passage slowly or carefully and prayerfully, asking the guidance and inspiration of the Holy Spirit.

2. Jesus before the Eyes

As the words bring before one the presence of Jesus in His words and deeds, use the mind and imagination to note every detail. Use some Bible notes or commentary to help focus attention on Jesus in the days of His flesh.

3. Jesus in the Heart

As you watch the Jesus of yesterday, realise that He is the *Jesus* of today in whom by sacrament and prayer you live now. He is as near to you as the disciples in the days of his *flesh*. Let Jesus be contemporary in heart and mind, imagination and will as all become engaged in the meditation, stimulating the affections into a deeper experience of his love.

4. Jesus in the Hands

As his disciple today what does this means for you? It may not be in the form of something to do, but in the form of a challenge to change into what He wants you to become.

Such methods outlined here are guidelines and must be used in a spirit of flexibility and not the fixity of something rigid, for it is the Holy Spirit that is the source and inspiration of our prayer, not a logical pattern of thought. Therefore as St Francis de Sales says, sometimes after preparation one finds one's affections stirred up towards God. At this moment he tells us that they should be allowed free rein, without trying to follow the method at all. Normally consideration of the subject for meditation preceded affections and resolutions, but the Holy Spirit might well give us affections before the consideration. Therefore miss out the consideration because its purpose is to stir up the affections. This is not to give way to whim or instability, but to the promptings of the Holy Spirit. The method then becomes a guideline rather than an inflexible yoke which even God is not allowed to disturb.

The classical teaching of methods of meditation cautions us against confusing the method itself as the prayer. All methods of meditation are concerned to draw our dispersed human powers together, quieting some down and engaging others, so that when prayer begins to flow of itself we should let it lead us. If we need a method to lead us into prayer, and most people do when they begin to meditate, then choose one, which conforms to our own psychological and temperamental type. The reflective and analytical mind will find it needs a method of the Ignatian type, while the more intuitive person will tend to feel more at home with the methods which stem from the seventeenth-century French Oratory or more akin to that of Eastern Orthodoxy. Whatever way one goes one must realise that the purpose of the method is not to have beautiful thoughts or striking intuitions about God, but to enter into converse and communion with Him.

9

Silence and Praying

Gather yourself together in the heart, and there practise secret meditation. By this means, with the help of God's grace, the spirit of zeal will be maintained in its true character – burning sometimes less and sometimes more brightly. Secret meditation sets our feet on the path of inner prayer which is the most direct road to salvation. We may leave all else and turn only to this work, and all will be well. Conversely, if we fulfil all other duties and neglect this one task we shall bear no fruit.

Bishop Theophan

There is a growing interest in the use of silence as a way of praying, the way of quiet waiting upon God, commonly known as contemplative prayer. In *Sacred and Secular* Bishop Michael Ramsey asked whether the movements to recover the true meaning of liturgy, the bridging of the gap between worship and the common life, would succeed, 'unless there is with them a revival of contemplative prayer'. He saw 'some significant signs of a new discovery of contemplative prayer, the prayer of quiet waiting upon God in the setting of everyday life'. Since the publication of his Holland Lectures in 1964 there has been a tremendous surge towards mysticism, the craving for a mystical element in the lives of a growing number of people.

Contemplative prayer is the prayer of hunger and thirst, of desire for God, be the desire, strong or very feeble. It is the prayer in which the self is not pious but simply itself towards reality and God and in which the images and sophistications both of religion and irreligion are left behind as a person finds in the depth of himself One whom he desires. Such is the prayer, which links Christianity and ordinary life.

In *Contemplative Prayer,* Thomas Merton explains that such seeking of God is not a matter of our finding him by means of certain methods and ascetic techniques. It is rather a quieting of our whole life by self-denial, prayer and good works, so that God himself, who seeks us more than we seek him, can 'find us' and 'take possession of us'. He goes on to say that we must realise our nothingness and emptiness, which requires a complete surrender of the exterior, the false self, to God's love. We must let go of everything that is centred on the illusory false self and thus gain the truer self that is the image of God within us. God's love will fill the emptiness.

Such a way of knowing God, by allowing oneself to become receptive in a quiet waiting upon him, is, as the mystics have attested and Michael Ramsey has pointed out, 'accessible to any man, woman or child who is ready to try to be obedient and humble and to want God very much'.

The Way of the Pilgrim

The experience described in *The Way of the Pilgrim* has a contemporary ring about it. Like many a twentieth-century seeker this simple man wants to find out how to pray without ceasing, having heard during the Liturgy the passage from St Paul encouraging him to pray in this way. The book tells the story of a Russian pilgrim who spent a year searching for the secret of such unceasing prayer before meeting a monk to whom he mentions his desire for such prayer. The monk tells him that the heavenly light of unceasing interior prayer is found in poverty of spirit and in active experience in simplicity of heart. Many people, the monk tells him, get it the wrong way round. They think that good actions and all sorts of preliminary measures render us capable of prayer. Actually, it is the reverse which is true. It is prayer, which bears fruit in good works and all the virtues. The Christian is bound to perform many good works, but before all else what he ought to do is pray, for without prayer no other good work whatever can be accomplished.

> Unceasing prayer is the mother of all spiritual blessings. 'Capture the mother' said St. Isaac, and she will bring you the children. Learn first to acquire the power of prayer and you will easily practise all the virtues.' The monk tells the pilgrim that those who know little of this from practical experience and the profoundest teaching of the Holy Fathers, have no clear knowledge of it and speak of it little.

When they reached the monastery the pilgrim implored the monk to show him what praying without ceasing meant and how it could be learned. So the monk continued and told him that the continuous interior prayer of Jesus is a constant calling upon the divine name of Jesus, with the lips, in the Spirit, in the heart. In this calling on the Holy Name the pilgrim is to form a mental picture of his constant presence and implore his grace, at all times and in all places, even during sleep. The words to be used are these:

> *Lord Jesus Christ, Son of God, have mercy on me a*
> *sinner*

If the pilgrim accustoms himself to the constant repetition of this prayer, he will experience so deep a consolation and so great a need always to offer this prayer, that he can no longer live without it. Eventually it will continue to voice itself in him of its own accord. The pilgrim asks the monk to teach him how to gain the habit of this continual prayer. He gives him a book for that slow meditative reading mentioned earlier. It is entitled *The Philokalia*, which means love of the beautiful, the exalted, the good, and is a collection of sayings of the Fathers of the Eastern Church. In these sayings is contained an interpretation of the secret life in Our Lord Jesus Christ, which is the true Christian life. The sayings have been described as small nuggets of instruction. The monk read one of these sayings from St Symeon the New Theologian:

Sit down alone and in silence. Lower your head, shut your eyes, breathe out gently and imagine yourself looking into your own heart. Carry your mind, that is your thoughts, from your head into your heart. As you breathe out say, 'Lord Jesus Christ, have mercy on me.' Say it moving your lips gently or simply say it in your mind. Try to put all thoughts aside. Be calm, be patient and repeat the process very frequently.

The Jesus Prayer

The prayer the monk gave to the pilgrim is known as the *Jesus Prayer*, the calling on the name of Jesus. It has a long history going back to the early centuries of the Church, but in principle reaching back much further into the biblical tradition. In Old Testament times the recalling of the divine name was to bring one into an experience of the very presence of God himself. Hence the Jesus Prayer is entirely scriptural and expresses the reverence Christians have always had for the name of Jesus.

Though reduced to a single phrase or sentence the prayer contains two essential elements of Christian devotion, adoration and compunction. In the same moment as we are expressing our adoration to God in and through 'Lord Jesus Christ, Son of God', like the publican we also remember and give expression to our sorrow for human weakness in 'Lord have mercy on me a sinner'. The combination of what we think and feel as the divine name is prayerfully uttered gives our prayer its power. It is not magic that lies behind the prayer but the deep conviction that Jesus Christ, true God and true man, who died and was raised by God, still lives within us and leads us to share in his risen life. Our prayer is therefore centred on the divine Christ, convinced that he sees, hears and listens and whose presence we come to know and experience.

The Jesus Prayer is described as a prayer of simplicity whose aim is to help one enter into the heart and core of one's being, in order to encounter God through Jesus Christ and his indwelling Spirit in an interior way. First, begin by being recollected and inviting the inspiration of the Holy Spirit to establish the peace in your heart that is necessary for true prayer. Then recite the prayer slowly and quietly, saying each word with recollection, avoiding haste and without labouring. Alongside outer attention there must be an inner concentration that is relaxed and avoids the temptation to foster any artificiality of false emotion. To counter distraction, pause between the recitations of each phrase.

The prayer will develop in various stages. In the second stage it becomes more inward and acquires a rhythm of its own as the mind repeats it without any conscious act of the will. A further stage takes the prayer into the heart where it dominates the personality, its rhythm identifying with the movement of the heart and becoming unceasing. It leads us with God's grace and our own continued cooperation into incessant prayer. Growing into a way of incessant prayer requires a balanced and regular sacramental life, as the Jesus Prayer can never be a substitute for the Eucharist but only an added enrichment. It is essential to have a spiritual adviser if one is embarking on this way of prayer.

As we grow into this way of praying we will find that like the pilgrim we will be able to recite this short and simple prayer at any time in any place. It can be said in the bus queue, while working in the garden or kitchen, at the place of work, when dressing or walking and instead of counting sheep during the night when we cannot sleep. In moments of stress and mental strain when other ways of praying are impossible here is a way to pray. 'Wherever you go you are pregnant with Christ, and you bring his presence as you would bring the presence of a natural child.'

Silence and stillness

Despite some of the extravagances of his prayerful feats, the pilgrim soon realised that there was more to this way of unceasing prayer than mere recitation of a short phrase, and his pilgrimage was not going to be confined to the vast open spaces of the Russian countryside. More importantly it was going to be a pilgrimage into the unlimited expanses of his own 'inner space', to possess the pearl of great price, the kingdom of eternal life in the deep of his own heart. In *The Philokalia* he would read the words of Isaac the Syrian:

> Be at peace with your own soul, then heaven and earth will be at peace with you. Enter eagerly into the treasure house that is within you, and so you will see the things that are in heaven; for there is but one single entry to them both. The ladder that leads to the Kingdom is hidden within your soul. Flee from sin, dive into yourself, and in your soul you will discover the stairs by which to ascend.

Unlike the pilgrim who had the open spaces of Russia and St Isaac who had the solitude of the Syrian Desert, most of us have to live within the circumstances of home and family life in the workaday world. To run away from such responsibilities would only lead to false religion and unreality, because it is within these limited circumstances of life in which we have to live that God calls us to respond to the spiritual fullness of them. How can I find peace within them so that I find peace within myself, and heaven and earth makes peace with me? My life situation can be the instrument that leads me into authentic living and for most people this must be their 'desert', the place where they meet God in the daily round and common task of life's circumstances. Here is the field in which lies the pearl of great price. To possess it one must let go of everything that is preventing one from having it. To enter into such knowledge and experience of God's kingdom will require a way of living in which there is time for silence and prayer. Like the pilgrim it will mean establishing in one's own life the personal equivalent to his times of withdrawal into silence, turning aside from the distracting noise of life and seeking God in silence.

The first requirement is to find a space within the daily round of life's routine when in silence and solitude one can come apart to quietly wait on God. It may be difficult to find this desert place in which to wait and listen to God. When in that place and time of prayer it will be even more difficult to find the 'desert place' within, that interior tranquillity of heart in which to listen and hear God. Yet it is for this that we come apart, to separate ourselves so that we may enter into an interior silence of the heart. Here we discover that most of the noise is on the inside, a noise that comes from the broken, fragmented and distracted parts of ourselves which are always seeking their own self-centred expression. Silence is not something that just happens. It is a long pilgrimage during which we have to allow God to integrate and co-ordinate these distracted elements into an interior tranquillity and peace.

When we become still and quiet new discoveries are made about parts of ourselves, either previously unknown or thought to have disappeared, as the silence allows parts of the real self to surface from the subconscious to the conscious mind. We begin to see ourselves as we really are in the noises that fragment and distract our spirit; the things that 'bump' us awake in the night. They appear in the form of anxieties agitating thoughts and desires, the tensions between the pain of real life and the imagined joy that our dreams and fantasies bring. Alongside these are the noises created in us by the people we find difficult, the things on our consciences, the conflicts and tensions of life. Thomas Merton advised that before thinking about contemplation, there must be a recovery of one's basic natural unity, a reintegration of one's compartmentalised being into a co-ordinated and simple whole. One has to learn to live as a unified human person. This means bringing back together those fragments of one's distracted existence, so that when one says 'I' there is really something present to support the pronoun that has been uttered.

Inner silence

The second requirement is the pilgrimage into an inner silence, a journey into the discovery of one's real self, alongside which one will see the false self 'I have always imagined was really me'. Again Merton pointed out that, 'Before we can realise who we really are, we must become conscious of the fact that the person we think we are here and now, is at least an impostor and a stranger'. Merton goes on to say that the false self, what he calls the empirical ego, is illusory, a mask for our true identity, our true self, which is the deepest self in which we stand naked before God. Solitude and prayer help strip us of this false self since there is no need of a fabrication before God who knows us through and through. We have to 'let go' of it as we face and acknowledge ourselves as we really are in a positive penitence that discovers a need for more simple dependence upon God.

God calls us to 'let go' of those things in our lives, in our very being, that diffuse and distract us away from him, to 'let go' of our control on those parts of ourselves, those parts of our lives. With so much self-emptying it becomes apparent why the monk should tell the pilgrim that the heavenly light of unceasing interior prayer is found in poverty of spirit and in active experience in simplicity of heart. This way of prayer is described as a way of poverty, because we have to allow so much within us that is an obstacle to God's grace to be emptied out. Only then can we grow into that condition of life described in the Beatitudes, 'the poor in spirit', which is a blessing. The initiative comes from God, as we remain still and quiet and receptive to him in a spirit of love and self-surrender, allowing the distracted parts of ourselves to be cleansed and unified in a stillness that must come through the uprising of love, the desire to be wholly God's. It is a Gethsemane moment when the false self must be allowed to die and the real self is purified, cleansed, and reconciled to the Father.

When this happens God consoles us in an experience in which we intuitively know that God loves us. Such an experience of being-loved-by-God at such a deep level of our consciousness restores our strength, and brings with it a childlike trust, joy and peace in the embrace of the indwelling God. It is a gift from God's Spirit, the reward of the heavenly Father to those who enter their inner chamber to pray in secret. St Paul described the fruit of such silence of the heart as 'love, joy, peace, patience, kindness, goodness, trustfulness, gentleness and self-control'. When you make peace with your own soul, heaven and earth make peace with you.

Disposition

To enter into this kind of inward knowledge and experience is not something that we can contrive. It is a gift of
God given to those who wait receptively in stillness and
silence, a gift of the Holy Spirit who prays within us
without our words but with God's single unspoken Word.
Within this inner centre of motivation and love one sees
oneself and everything else in a new light. It requires the
rooting of oneself in worship and prayer and the putting
of oneself unconditionally at the disposal of God. Inward
knowledge and the disposition of coming to God unconditionally are closely linked. Unconditional means being
ready to be stripped of the 'hang ups' that push and impel
and thereby prevent one from being free; the intellectual
'hang ups' of one's own presuppositions, the psychological 'hang ups' that rattle like dried skeletons in the
cupboards of our memories, and the spiritual 'hang ups'
in the 'sins that do so easily beset us'. They veil and distort
the real sense of existence suggesting and impelling one
like a machine into the triviality of purposeless behaviour.
One uses them to cover and hide oneself from God
because of the fear of appearing before him naked. Yet to
stand and wait before God in the silence of utter nakedness beyond the barricades of one's 'hang ups' is what
coming before God unconditionally means. The purpose
of all this is so that one may listen to God. 'The voice of
God is heard' says Gregory the Great, 'when with minds at
ease, we rest from the bustle of the world and the divine
precepts are pondered by us in the silence of the heart.'
This is a silence that embraces not only the conscious
levels of our being but the unconscious as well.

When we rest from the bustle of the world we soon
realise that most of the noise and bustle comes from
within. A kind of 'inner warfare' explodes into consciousness revealing the lack of peace, of silence and stillness in
our own hearts. Inevitably it distracts and diffuses our
prayer. This is what the Abbot Isaac told John Cassian
when in the fourth century he and his friend Germanus
went to him and asked him to teach them to pray.

The mind at prayer, said the Abbot, is as it was made to be before the time of prayer. When we dispose ourselves to prayer, the image of the same actions, words and feelings, will flit before our eyes, and reproducing what has gone before, will make rise in us either feelings of anger or depression or will cause us to go over again past desires and business.

If God is to reveal himself in the depth of one's being, and one is to hear God in Gregory's sense, one must flee from noise through both interior and exterior silence. 'Whatever we would not have our minds to entertain when we are at prayer', says Abbot Isaac, 'let us before the hour of prayer hasten to expel from the secret places of our hearts.' Herein, says St Basil, is that beginning of the purified heart, the necessary precondition for seeing God whose purpose is to allow silence to create a space, emptiness in the depths of one's being where God can be heard without any other noise. Such silence is an expression of our poverty, the emptiness that remains after we have freely and fully accepted the 'letting go' of so much in us that causes the noise. Just as there is a kind of silence that springs from our 'poverty of spirit', so there is another kind of silence that springs from fullness within. It is born from the experience of the fullness of God's presence that has filled our emptiness and in which true contemplation is born. In such silence the heart rests and reposes as it senses the sweetness and wonders of contemplation. The silence is prayer witnessing to the fullness of the life of God within us, a fullness, which must renounce all human words in order to express it adequately.

For a while, maybe only the words of the Bible are used, or perhaps the name of Jesus until the moment comes when silence alone can express the extraordinary richness in our heart. This silence enfolds a person gently and powerfully and always comes from within where prayer governs it and teaches us when we should be silent and when we should speak. While it is pure praise, at the same time it radiates out towards others. Such silence never hurts anyone for it establishes a zone of peace and quiet around the one who is silent, where God can be irresistibly felt as present. 'Keep your heart in peace' says

St Seraphim of Sarov, 'and a multitude around you will be saved.'

This silence brings one into that state of tranquillity in which all inordinate movements and desires, passions and thoughts are quelled. Silence is not completely real until it expresses the depths of our being, disposing us into that condition in which we are more able and ready to listen and know God. In such stillness and tranquillity we surrender ourselves totally to God, dwelling and revealing himself in this temple of God, which is me. We pass beyond our normal habit of reasoning about God and our duties towards him and discover as we open ourselves beyond the 'hang ups' that have hitherto controlled our responses, God, whose presence instantly destroys the idols we have often mistaken for him. C. S. Lewis made this point to Malcolm:

> Only God himself, can let the bucket down into the depths of us. And on the other side he must constantly work as the iconoclast. Every idea of him we form, he must in mercy shatter. The most blessed result of prayer would be to rise thinking, 'But I never knew before, I never dreamed ...' I suppose it was at such a time that Thomas Aquinas said of all his theology 'it reminds me of straw'.[1]

A cell of solitude

Our aim must be to build a cell within, the type of cell where solitude reigns, the inner chamber in which tranquillity is experienced and the presence of God known. Here we come face to face with our true self and God in an unconditional nakedness, 'a nudity of the spirit', open, receptive, and without preconceived ideas of what God the Blessed Trinity will reveal. If prayer is the quality of a presence spontaneously shared, we must move beyond the games we play to avoid losing control. We must wait and be ready to meet God on his terms hoping to receive him as he wishes to make himself known. Here with the

---

[1] C. S. Lewis, *Letters to Malcolm*, London, Geoffrey Bles, 1964, p. 109.

mind in the heart we discover the truth that sets us free, not as an object of knowledge to be possessed, but as the person of the Blessed Trinity by whom we are possessed. He it is who frees us in a salvation that is more than mere forgiveness but a genuine renewal of our whole being. We inwardly experience the mystery of living in the Trinity, a mutual indwelling of love and life shared between the divine persons and ourselves. The Spirit, St Irenaeus says, comes to seize us and give us to the Son, and the Son gives us to the Father. 'If anyone loves me' says Jesus, 'we will come to him and make in him our abode.'

In this cell of solitude life is to be grounded in the life the Father shares with the Son in the Holy Spirit. It is a partaking of divine life, where silence is absolutely necessary if we are to be sensitive to the interior Word the Holy Spirit speaks in the heart. This cell of stillness in which we come to live, we are to carry with us everywhere. As the person who lives in it we are becoming a person who listens, ever more sensitive to the Word of God in Scripture and life.

The single verse

In this cell of solitude where the presence of God is known and experienced, the advice of John Cassian is wise counsel to follow. He advises the reducing of our prayer to a single short phrase to be repeated continuously. The mind throws out and represses the rich and ample matter of all thoughts and restricts itself 'to the poverty of the single verse'. Such a single verse is the Jesus Prayer. Psalm 46 verse 10, 'Be still and know that I am God' is another. The words should be repeated continuously but with feeling, faithfully and lovingly. The sole sound will be the sound of this phrase rather like a harmonic within us, building up a resonance that leads us forward to our own wholeness. In the slow and deliberate repetition of this verse we hold ourselves still in the realisation of the presence of God in Christ. Instead of thinking about him or trying to see him refracted through our imagination, we brood on the truth that he actually is present to us and nearer to us than the air we breathe. So the heart becomes absorbed in attending to this stupendous truth; that he is as present to us as he was to his first followers. Our prayer is more than mere attention to this truth of God's presence. It is an experience of it in which the *self* is suitably forgotten. Our consciousness becomes inevitably like that on which we have gazed and obedient to that to which we have listened, as we become one in a union of love with the subject of our knowing. Our knowledge goes beyond knowledge about and becomes an inward knowledge or love-knowledge that is nothing less than an experience of the very reality of the presence of God in the heart.

Here we open ourselves in a receptivity and obedience, listening rather than giving, commanding, or speaking, that is not a passive condition, but the consciousness and realisation that our acts do not originate in ourselves, but are drawn out and inspired by acts of God. Such inspiration will effect in us a radical change of heart and mind which brings new vision, but only in so far as we are willing to die in order that we might live. For the experience, in so far as there is nothing blocking the response, cleanses and awakens our adoration and love so that resolutions are not needed. Our consciousness, awakened and touched by this living Presence, receives from him an infusion of life and issues spontaneously in thoughts and actions rising from this change of feeling in this communion and prayer.

> Be at peace, with your own soul, enter eagerly into the treasure house that is within you and so you see the things that are in heaven.

A life not a technique

Prayer is not a technique, a theory, or a method. It is a way of life at the centre of which is God, the Blessed Trinity. It is a life centred in him and is caught from constant nearness to him and the prayer, in which the continual recollection of the holy presence of God is primary, is a disposition of life rather than the perfect performance of a technique. This life is rooted in the sacraments, a Eucharistic life, where in disposing oneself towards God the prayer of Jesus is allowed to rise in our hearts. This was the spirit of the Abbot Isaac's advice to John Cassian. He did not introduce him to some predetermined doctrine and practice, but to a way of life that was to be caught from constant nearness to God in the continued recollection of his presence. Hence, Cassian can say that our practical perfection depends on first knowing the nature of our faults, and secondly finding out the order of the virtues and forming our characters by striving to perfect ourselves in them.

Here the *Pascha Christi*, the death and resurrection of Christ, must be allowed to take hold on one's life and transform it. One must lose one's life in order to find it in the emptying out of unreality and artificiality, laying down one's life in the poverty of the single verse, 'letting go' of everything, that in a poverty of spirit one might see the Kingdom of God. Tito Colliander explains it like this:

> You should see yourself as a child who is setting out to learn the first sounds of letters, and who is taking the first tottering steps. All worldly wisdom and all the skills you have are totally worthless in the warfare that awaits you and equally without value are your social standing and your Possessions.
>
> Property that is not used in the Lord's service is a burden and knowledge that does not engage the heart is barren and therefore harmful because presumptuous. It is called naked, for it is without warmth and fosters no love.
>
> You must thus abandon your knowledge and become a dunce in order to become wise; you must become a pauper in order to be rich and a weakling if you wish to be strong.[2]

One's search is for the true self and the experience of one's own personal and infinite capacity to be known and loved by God. That real self lies beyond all selfishness and can only be known in God as part of the 'inward knowledge'. But to arrive at it one must enter into a radical

---

2. Tito Colliander, The Way of the Ascetics, London and Southhampton, Hodder and Stroughton, 1960, p. 24.

experience of personal poverty in the surrendering of the false image that one has come to regard as one's true self, along with all the unreality this has created in one's life. Discovering that one is not what imagined oneself to be is a painful experience, the pain being in proportion to the extent that one has taken the illusions about oneself to be real. All such artificiality crumbles as one concentrates, attends to and waits on God, whose light of truth illuminates the true self filling it not only with a sense of nothingness before the beauty of God, but bringing the kind of brokenness in spirit, the contrite heart of the poor in spirit which is a blessing, for theirs is the kingdom of heaven.

In St Augustine's language we have found the stepping stone that will lead to God, in the real self, which becomes the sacrifice of one's broken and contrite heart which knows God will not despise. The silence into which God calls us is an interior condition of humility and poverty, beyond what normally conditions us in the senses, emotions and affections, so that we may be free to say 'Yes' to him with our very being. Such an experience goes beyond words, pious phrases and sentiments, even beyond thought itself. God calls us to rest and 'taste' in a condition of living communion with him in the continuous response of our being. Here the words of T. S. Eliot ring true:

> Prayer is more
> Than an order of words, the conscious occupation
> Of the praying mind, or the sound of the voice praying.

It is looking upon God in pureness of heart rather like a baby looking on his father's or mother's face. Certainly it is as natural as that, this waiting, looking and resting in the security of an experience, the experience of one's whole being tasting the very presence of one whose love meets one in an embrace of peace. Just as there is dialogue between mother and baby in their loving embrace, a dialogue not of words but of love, so too in this high point of prayer, dialogue with God is not in terms of a wordy conversation, but in terms of being held in the loving embrace of God communicating a life that words would only faintly express. One is drawn into assimilation with God that convinces one that one no longer lives to oneself but that God lives in one and one lives in God. 'Eye has not seen, nor ear heard ... nor has it entered into the heart of man to conceive what God has prepared for those who love him.'

New psychic and spiritual powers grow, released through the energies of God that have touched our consciousness. One passes over the abyss that lies between merely thinking and actually seeing, between knowledge about things and immediate perception of things. Such 'inward knowledge' is different from the knowledge our minds bring to us. It is the fruit of letting ourselves be possessed by God in an experience in which we intuitively know that God loves us. It brings healing, consolation and peace, restores our strength and gives a childlike trust, joy and peace in the embrace of the indwelling Trinity. Such a sense of God becomes the presupposition of all our thinking, the centre of motivation and love, and determines how we live.

10

Holy Scripture and Prayer

Lectio divina *means 'divine reading'. At first sight that idea may seem simple, but in fact it is both deep and rich. The adjective* divina *shows that we are not dealing here with any kind of reading. Certainly it is not profane reading; it provides neither erudition nor mere amusement. But it is also something more than what might be called pious or edifying reading. It is even more than spiritual reading, in the sense in which this phrase is used today. It is called divine because in it God gives us His Word directly. It is not, a matter of reading 'things about God; God takes the initiative and intervenes in person'. In* lectio divina *God speaks to and addresses each person individually, and the reader must give himself as best he can to the Word of God.*

George Cronk
The Message of the Bible

Lectio divina

In giving oneself to the prayer of contemplation Holy Scripture will become more immediately alive with meaning as it becomes the nourishment and inspiration of such prayer. We have seen that prayer is not some esoteric exercise outside the community of faith. In the communal prayer of the Eucharist our participation in Word and Sacrament provides the living context in which we proclaim the fact of God's redeeming work and become more identified with it. Also, there is a need for regular disciplined reading of Holy Scripture whose primary aim is not mere pious edification, not just to read things about God, but to dispose ourselves to wait and listen for God to take the initiative and intervene in person and give us his Word directly, speaking and addressing 'me' as I give myself as best I can to the Word of God. *Lectio* divina means 'divine reading', the adjective divina signifying that this is not any kind of reading. It provides neither erudition nor mere amusement and is something more than merely edifying reading or spiritual reading. It is called divine because God gives us his Word directly, so that it is not merely reading things about God but God coming and speaking directly to each person individually. So I come not only as a reader but also as a listener to hear especially with the heart. Even when the preoccupations of life in the workaday world prevent me from reading the text of Scripture, there are those scriptural passages retained in the memory. These can keep one ruminating on God's Word when preoccupied with workaday life and become part of the unceasing prayer that goes on in the heart.

This approach to the Word of God does not expect some pre-programmed result as if what is going to happen depends on our own effort. Here we come to God through his Word by submitting ourselves to his control and power, allowing it not only to create something new but also to disturb like a 'two-edged sword', to awaken and restore us to newness of life. If the heart is the place where God comes and makes his 'abode' with those who love him, then it is with an openness that we must listen if we want to hear the Word of God. Like Mary who pondered so many things in her heart, we must learn the discipline of discerning the Word that can pierce our souls too. Reading and listening to God's Word with the heart requires a discernment that only interior prayer can bring. It will take us beyond the rational and imaginative ways of knowing that are not equal to this task into the realm of vision and perception.

This is not to dismiss the historico-critical method as expendable in the life of prayer, but to point out that to

get to the 'marrow of God's Word', a more complete
approach is necessary. It is not a denial of the need and
usefulness of the historical and literary knowledge the crit-
ical method brings to the interpretation of God's Word for
today. In a more complete approach to the Word of God,
it is the necessary prelude of preparation, after which,
without commentary, in a stillness of mind and imagination or poverty of spirit, we rest before God in quiet attention. We wait attentively for this poverty or emptiness to
be filled with the richness and power of God's Word. This
gradual process demands patient perseverance and humility as we wait in faith and trust, allowing the desire for the
Lord our God to be nurtured within. Such a waiting on
Scripture can be difficult, especially before the word of
Scripture has become life-giving and the natural tendency
is to enlighten and warm the heart by retreating into the
suggestive thoughts of reason and imagination. This temptation must be resisted, as we persistently wait in an attentive stillness and silence for the Word of God to speak in
our heart. We wait for that Word of God, which is alive and
active, to cut through to where soul and spirit meet.

> Our heart is the place of God . . . This word comes to bring it
> life, and filled with this life the heart stirs and awakens. The
> power of God, which is in his word, strikes it and makes it
> vibrate and echo to the very life of God. The word seeks out our
> heart and then our heart seizes on the word of God. The two
> recognize each other. In this first blinding by the word of God,
> our heart truly hears the word and in that same instant recog-
> nizes itself as a new being, recreated before God in the very
> power of his word. Henceforth things will never be the same. A
> new doorway has been opened. A crucial threshold has been
> crossed. A new criterion of discernment has been given to us.
> Having once recognized God's power in his word, so unlike all
> other inward experiences, we recognize it again when it comes
> to us, just as we can thereafter detect its absence.[1]

The Psalter will become our prayer book par excellence,
the word awakening the heart and creating a sensitivity to

[1.] Dom André Louf, *The Cistercian Alternative*, Dublin, Gill & Macmil-
lan, 1983, p. 78.

the life of God within. Increasing numbers of people are rediscovering the Psalms and using them in their solitary prayer. Their familiar recurring phrases shape the subconscious as well as the conscious mind, creating the attitudes of repentance and need. Using them in this way leads one to discover the richness of this deeply human prayer book, where the failure of the human condition is brought to the mercy and faithfulness of God. The two themes running through the Psalter, the glory of God in praise and thanksgiving and the need of man in the penitential psalms, find their conjunction in us by virtue of Baptism and thereby are brought into the whole reconciliation in Christ. Reciting the Psalms daily and using them contemplatively directly effects our own conversion, our understanding of our need of God's love and contributes to our life in Christ, not always consciously but as the underlying ground of our prayer. The Psalms occupy an altogether special place in the Bible. Like all the other books, the Psalter contains the word of God.

> But the word of God in the psalms has changed its direction. It not only comes from God, it returns to him through the human heart. It is a word which God puts on man's lips so that by it he may unerringly invoke God. The psalmist had to have a heart impregnated by the word of God for this miracle to happen. God's word become prayer went out from him to return to God after recreating the psalmist's heart.[2]

When the heart is awakened, it is not so much the attentiveness to the words that matters, but the attentive hearing and listening to the heart. It is of this movement of our own hearts that these words speak. Furthermore, they speak of the larger context of God's activity in the history of salvation and his will for the whole world. An experience described by Canon Allchin hints at what this can mean. It was at Mattins in a Greek monastery. One of the Psalms with which the Byzantine Rite begins is Psalm 63. The Abbot recited the Psalms: 'O God, thou art my God; early will I seek thee. My soul thirsteth for thee, my flesh also longeth after thee: in a barren and dry land where no water is.'

[2.] Louf, *The Cistercian Alternative*, p. 98.

I said the Abbot would recite the psalms. But that gives the wrong impression. He spoke them as if they were being spoken for the first time, speaking them from the depths of his heart; and yet at the same time speaking them with the weight of almost three thousand years, a hundred generations of longing after God. It was as if the whole tradition was speaking through him. Scripture comes to fulfilment when it ceases to be Scripture and becomes living speech. The Spirit who breathed in the original psalmist breathed in the man who now spoke the psalmist's words. They were words filled with the Spirit. One saw something about the presence of the past, about the self-renewing nature of tradition.[3]

A clue to using the Psalms contemplatively is given by John Cassian in his Xth Coherence. Here he advises the practice of using the single short phrase to achieve the stillness necessary for prayer. A daily reading of the Psalms should not only feed and identify the heart and mind with the statements of the Psalter, but also provide a fund of single verses upon which to ruminate in times of contemplative stillness. The purpose of the single verse is to bring us to the realisation that in essence our aim is to so dispose ourselves that the prayer of Jesus might arise in our hearts. Hence the verse must not only be in the heart at those times when one consciously enters into stillness and silence but, wrote Cassian,

> must always be in the heart, till having been moulded by it you grow accustomed to repeat it even in your sleep. On rising it should anticipate all your waking thoughts, and throughout the day it should be singing ceaselessly in the recesses of your heart .

Such prayer is to allow God's mysterious and silent presence within us to become more and more the reality, which gives meaning and shape and purpose to all we do, to everything we are. Carl Jung was once asked in an interview whether he believed in God. After a pause he quietly, said 'No, I know'. Cassian touches on this reality of direct experience as the fruit of contemplation. He tells us that in reading the Psalms we no longer just read them or

[3.] A. M. Allchin, *The Dynamic of Tradition*, London, DLT, 1981, pp. 27–8.

memorise them. We come to get at their meaning, not by reading the text but by experiencing and anticipating it. This is the essence of what Thomas Merton says of the Saints and Fathers:

> They did not simply consider the psalm as they passed over it, drawing from it some pious reflection. They entered into the 'action' of the psalm. They allowed themselves to be absorbed in the spiritual agony of the Psalmist and of the God whom he represented. They allowed their sorrows to be swallowed up in the sorrows of this mysterious Personage and then they found themselves swept away on the strong tide of his hope into the very depths of God.[4]

He goes on to say that we too find out that,

> when we bring our own sorrows and desires and hopes and fears to God, and plunge them all into the sorrows and hopes of the mysterious One who sings the psalm, a kind of transubstantiation is effected. We have put all we have or rather all our poverty, all that we have not, into the hands of Christ. He who is Everything and has everything, pronounces over our gifts words of his own. Consecrated with the poverty he assumed to deliver us, we find that in his poverty our poverty becomes infinite riches; in his sufferings our defeats are transubstantiated into victories and his death becomes our everlasting life.[5]

What has happened? We have been transformed far more deeply than anything psychological. There is something much deeper. It is a spiritual solution, a transformation operated in us by the Holy Spirit who lives and acts in the world he has inspired.

> The peculiar mystical impact with which certain verses of the psalms suddenly produce this silent depth-change in the heart of the contemplative is only to be accounted for because we, in the Spirit, recognize the Spirit singing in ourselves.[6]

[4.] Thomas Merton, *Bread in the Wilderness*, London, Catholic Book Club, 1953, pp. 66–7.
[5.] Ibid., p. 67.
[6.] Ibid., p. 68.

We are transformed in the midst of God's discovery of himself in his own psalm. The Word of God is full of the Word of God. And the Christ who is born to us of Scripture is recognised because his Spirit recognises him in us, illuminating our minds and hearts with his secret presence.

In whispering this single word a very dense interior silence gradually arises and in it God makes himself present. Then we will no longer pronounce the word as such, but will rather hear and listen in the depths of our heart to what is spoken by another. This is the voice of the Spirit of God praying in us with inarticulate groans. All we need to do is abandon ourselves and give ourselves with the most interior faculties of our being to the presence of the Holy Spirit within us. When that happens we are truly children of God and led by the Spirit. Our prayer will be none other than the prayer of the Spirit, the prayer of the Son to his Father. In this prayer we shall find again the very source of our being, that secret entrance deep within us, which opens like a chasm to allow us to come to intimacy with God. There deep in that treasure house of the heart we shall find the ladder that leads to the kingdom.

The Bible

What John Cassian says about the Psalms, getting at their meaning not by reading the text but by experiencing and anticipating it, is similar to what he says about Scripture. The sense of Holy Scripture is revealed not by a commentary but by what he calls practical proof, because our own experience exposes the very veins and marrow of the Word of God. Hence the Bible stands alongside the Psalter as the reservoir that will irrigate our prayer. In private and corporate reading of Scripture, the words can be sacramental as we recall God's mighty acts in the history of his people. We are coming before God making anamnesis, remembrance, and giving thanks for what he has done. The element of conversion is not absent as we read of the long return to the Father accomplished by the People of God in the Old and New Testaments, and which must be accomplished in each Christian. The acts of God's mercy are read, the need of man is acknowledged, and this is the vital part of the accomplishment of the mystery of Christ in each one of us.

The problem of the interpretation is not the finding of some key with which to extract from the Word of Scripture, either some particular doctrine or the meaning of the Gospel for today. Rather does it rest on the faith of the Church that in the Scriptures God speaks to his Church. The faith which the Scriptures express and which the Church offers us and to which she leads us, kindles the light of the Holy Spirit in the heart of the believer. The Scriptures are part of the Tradition, which does not hold the Church captive to the past, but is something in which the Christian must live and move as the surest guide to the future. The scriptural Tradition is no formula, no form of words, but a continuity of life, mystical and sacramental; the mystery of Christ to which the Scriptures bear witness. Herein is the Rule of Faith which defines the Church and in accordance with which Scripture must be interpreted. At the heart of the Faith is a mystery that is lived, a continuity of life that claims the whole man. The apprehension of this mystery is not simply a cerebral activity but comes in ways that are unfathomable, because the mystery draws out our faith and love. That mystery is Christ, Therefore it is not just a question of believing the right things, not even, simply hearing the Word of Christ. More deeply it is a question of being with him at the deepest level in prayer. 'He who truly possesses the word of Jesus', says St Ignatius of Antioch, 'can also hear his stillness, that he may be perfect, that he may act through what he says, that he may be known through his silence.'

'Before any articulation of our confession of Christ', writes Andrew Louth, 'there is an articulate closeness to Christ, to that creative silence out of which the Word comes, to that stillness in which are wrought the mysteries that cry out.'[7] So we do not subordinate Scripture to the

7. Andrew Louth, 'The Hermeneutical Question Approached through the Fathers' in Sobornost 7/7/78. I have acknowledged my indebtedness to this article in my book *Towards a Renewed Priesthood*, Leominster, Gracewing, 1995, p. 89.

articulated faith of the Church, but listen to Scripture from a contemplative stillness that is being with Christ. This is something given and known in the life of the Church, in the Tradition which is the movement of the Spirit in the Church. This contemplative approach to Scripture is found in the Early Fathers but also in such mystics as Aelred of Rievaulx, Richard of St Victor, St Bernard and others. These men lived in a scriptural atmosphere and being saturated with the spirit of the Bible their thoughts were moulded by it. By constant communion of heart and mind with the Divine Presence they attained a deeply religious understanding of man's problems and the divine plan of salvation. Their spiritual insight into Scripture discovered the sacred history of the human race and the indiviual soul's spiritual journey, and they recognised there the soul's ascent to God. They drank from the divine wellspring and so read the Bible under the Spirit who inspired it. This explains why they could discover, as if by instinct, the true meaning of the text, for their minds were spontaneously in tune with the thought of the sacred books. They lived the reality, which their exegesis sought to discover behind the word.

But within this contemplative approach to Scripture was the conviction that Scripture allows of allegorical interpretation. In the spirit of St Paul, who contrasts shadow and reality for them, the sole reality is Christ and him whom we know through love. All else therefore is shadow, is allegory, and has value only in so far as it makes manifest the truth of the mystery of Christ. This recognises the fact that Scripture does not contain the whole truth, but only a partial reflection of it through which we might be enabled to discern the truth itself. Allegory is appropriate because it is not a definite method yielding clear and predictable results, but helping us to discern through Scripture a truth not contained in Scripture but witnessed to by it. In Scripture the truth is broken up so that we can grasp it and receive it as a gift and then look beyond it to the Giver, to Christ who is Truth.

Such an approach to Scripture is not scientific in the strict sense and is not meant to be. But it does have its canons of procedure. It is contemplative, it is a way of prayer, a living encounter of a life rooted in the mystery of Christ. Therefore it is not a simple matter of scriptural exposition, but much more. At a deeper level it is a matter of discernment, an alertness to the Word's disclosing of himself through the engagement with Scripture. Here we seek to see Scripture as a witness pointing to the Word, to Jesus Christ, in whose presence we live in the Spirit. It seeks to take us beyond the text to someone who could be captured by no text, to the Blessed Trinity. The task of listening to God which is prayer, in Scripture is just that, to listen to the Word speaking to us through Scripture, rather than piecing together some fragmentary witness of Scripture to make some construction of our own. In the end we pass beyond our own efforts, we let go our intellect and what we spin from it and simply listen.

We are not surrendering our reason to some arbitrary human convention. The Spirit and not our own ingenuity brings us to the meaning of Scripture the mystery of Christ revealing the Father. The understanding of Scripture is not a purely 'human affair'. The whole of revelation would be negated if the Spirit who inspired the prophets and apostles did not also move the hearts of believers to recognise and obey the Word of God speaking to them through their writings. This contemplative approach to Scripture in an openness to allegory is but an openness to God, to God's manifestation of himself in Scripture, so that we are responding to the mystery to which it is a witness. From this openness springs our apprehension of dogma and doctrine, the articulation of that stillness in the closeness of the mystery of Christ.

Fr George Moloney sums up the message of contemplation in these words,

> ... to the degree that one has purified and disciplined himself to sit before the Lord and listen to his Word, to that extent he can stand before the world and witness to the Word in loving service ... it teaches us the need to become prophets of the Word; meditating on the Word spoken in Scripture and re-lived in the mystery of the indwelling Trinity, we are sent forth as witnesses to that same existential Word being

spoken in the world as we yield ourselves to the process of bringing forth that Word in its fullness.[8]

This is the new life that the world needs, and indeed the Church. It is a life that is self-authenticating because it has its origin in a vision, the vision which is the fruit of the contemplative's prayer,

> Enkindle within us the fire of thy love
> And thou shalt renew the face of the earth.[9]

[8.] George Moloney, *The Breath of the Mystic*, New Jersey, Dimension Books, 1974, p. 38.
[9.] I have used material from chapter 5 of my book *Towards a Renewed Priesthood* where I have discussed contemplative living.

11

Icon of God

Man's basic need and ultimate purpose, then, is to become like God, to become one with God. Man was created for communion with God, and thus the final goal of human existence is participation 'in the fullness of the divine life'. 'To believe that man is made in God's image is to believe that man is created for communion and union with God, and that if he rejects this communion he ceases to be properly man' ... the process of moral and spiritual growth through which man may achieve union with God ... Fr Thomas Hopko defines as 'an unending process of growth and development' in which man becomes 'through gracious communion with God in freedom, all that God is by nature in the superabundant fulness of His inexhaustible and infinite Trinitarian being and life'.

George Cronk
The Message of the Bible

Man in his total being is created according to the divine image and likeness giving him a potential for a distinctive kind of life. 'The glory of God is a living man and the life of man is the vision of God' is how Irenaeus described it in the second century. To be truly human man must live in God and God in him, which the Incarnation demonstrated and this implies that to grow humanly means to grow spiritually and vice versa. Therefore to become a 'living man', that is fully human in Irenaeus's sense, requires that humankind respond to this potential for such a distinctive kind of life that God has given. Into each one of us God has built such potential and spiritual growth is the dynamic drawing out of this potential. God has created us in such a way that we know we are determined and conditioned by God, and in this fact we are truly human. The great spiritual masters of the Church define it in terms of man being made in the image of God and among these masters there is a basic conviction of the spiritual life as a progressive development of the image and likeness of God, from the moment of birth to the moment we die. The spiritual life is not something theoretical and abstract, but practical, a dynamic and concrete way of life in God, a constant movement from birth to the beatific vision. For them prayer is an experience of God in which they dynamically grow towards an ever-deepening awareness of living in the divine milieu and thereby partaking of the divine nature.

> God is always calling us to consent to be swept up into the Trinitarian life and we alone can reply. Our answer fulfils the purpose for which we were made or we destroy ourselves as human persons. This 'existential longing' to be what God wants us to be, in knowing and loving communication with him, is a spiritual thirst that is at the heart of being truly human. It is a yearning to become 'whole' and fulfilled. It is a longing that the image of God in man reach its full fruition.[1]

This way of understanding the spiritual life formed a universal tradition among the Early Fathers. Where the spirit of that tradition has been allowed to return in a concrete and life-giving way, it has led to impressive and life-giving renewal. One thinks of Aelred of Rievaulx and the great flowering of Cistercian life in England in the twelfth century. In the seventeenth century, St Francis de Sales, particularly through St John Chrysostom, finds in these early sources of spiritual doctrine the life-giving renewal that his own life needs, and through whom as bishop and spiritual counsellor God was to renew his Church.

It will at once be evident that the goal towards which

---

[1] George Moloney, *Invaded by God*, New Jersey, Dimension Books, 1979, p. 13.

human life needs to move is the realisation of our God-likeness in a living relationship with God, which is finally vision. Irenaeus, like all the Fathers, is quite unable to think of the life of the Spirit as a matter for theories and experiments divorced from the basic facts, which make its existence possible. The union of the human and the divine, which is a fact in the person of Christ, is a task to be achieved by people at large, and God's gesture of love in becoming man is both the sign of our destiny and the source of the only means of its fulfilment.

Spiritual growth in its fullness and perfection resides in assimilation to the likeness of Christ. Athanasius in the fourth century followed Irenaeus in claiming that God became man in order that man might become God. While this was meant literally it did not imply that we become God by nature but rather in the sense of the Second Letter of Peter, 'partakers of the divine nature'. 'We remain creatures' said Maximos the Confessor, 'while becoming God by grace'. Our assimilation is not to some kind of moral example outside ourselves, but to Christ, dynamically and ontologically living in us through grace. Grace is just that, not some objective gift given to us, but an encounter with the living Person whose life is in us. To live 'in Christ', means an organic union between Christ and the human person. That is the intention of Our Lord's high priestly prayer. 'May they all be one, as thou, Father art in me, and I in Thee, so also may they be one in us' (John 17:20).

In Christ then, God and man become one. In so far as a human being is 'in Christ' through faith and through full participation in the sacramental life of the Church, he is one with God, because Christ's humanity is one with God. Through the gracious work of the Holy Spirit the Christian believer is brought into an ever-developing and ever-deepening communion with God. The deification of the human person is a process of moral and spiritual growth toward God the Father, through God the Son, and in God the Holy Spirit, In this way, a person may become a 'partaker of the divine nature' (2 Peter 1:4), a participant in the energies and eternal life of the triune God.[2]

2. Moloney develops this theme in *Invaded by God*, pp. 43–62.

Living in the Trinity

Our devotional life, if it is to be Christian, must have its roots firmly planted in the central faith of the Blessed Trinity. To live in the sacramental life, in Baptism, Eucharist, and such other sacramental means of grace, is to live in the divine milieu of the Trinitarian life. There in God's presence and life the Christian grows into a greater consciousness of the divine presence conforming him to the likeness of his own image, the Christ in whom he lives.

The process of moving into a more conscious, loving relationship with God the Father, which means an onto-logical life living within man, is effected through the sanc-tifying activity of the Holy Spirit. St Cyril of Alexandria shows that these actions and operations of bringing man into the fullness of his powers are effected by the whole Trinity: 'All things come from the Father through the Son in the Holy Spirit'. Nothing of divine operation is attrib-uted to any Person of the Trinity unless it responds to the inter-Trinitarian relations.[3]

God's intention for each of us is, that always we are present to him, and this is the meaning of praying without ceasing. For prayer fructifies the divine life in which we live and assists our growth into that condition of life, whose sole aim is, in Julian of Norwich's language, a 'oneing' with the Blessed Trinity, the presence of persons of whom we become increasingly more conscious. Prayer is the key that unlocks the door into an experience of God in knowledge and love, our avenue into the eternal and boundless, the limitless, personal, and perfect love he has for each of us. Such prayer is real experience. We feel and taste God's love touching our consciousness in a renewing and recreating experience. In such a moment of disclosure there dawns the realisation that we are being grasped, known, and loved by God. Communication is not at the level of conversation. It is a communication in being, the drawing of us into inter-personal relationship with himself that we might partake of his own nature.

[3.] Moloney, *The Breath of the Mystic*, p. 120.

This is the promise Jesus gave when he said, 'If anyone loves me he will keep my word, and my Father will love him, and we shall come to him and make our home with him' (John 14:23). This was not beyond St Paul's experience when 'knowing the love of Christ, which is beyond all knowledge, you are filled with the utter fullness of God' (Eph. 3:19). Prayer draws us into a growing and ever-deepening consciousness of the Life the Father lives with the Son in the Holy Spirit, a life he wants us to share. We enter into the very movement of the Trinitarian life living within us,

> It is to swim in the powerful current of God's uncreated energies of love that completely surround us and permeate us as the ocean saturates a sponge. In such experiential prayer of the heart, we should not stop with mere feelings or affections or thoughts, but have the courage as the Spirit prompts us to pray in him, to move beyond pictures, images and even words. The Fathers of the desert constantly exhort us, as St. Gregory of Sinai summarizes it 'to force your mind to descend from the head to the heart and hold it there'.[4]

> Prayer becomes more and more a waiting in silence, a listening, a surrendering to the Holy Spirit who brings us to God's Word, that gives us knowledge that is beyond human knowledge, that brings us into darkness that is luminous. Only the Holy Spirit can reveal to us an experience of this divine triadic love. God is love (1 John 4:8), and this means that he is a community of . . . living Persons, his very being, his existence is to love. For God to be is to love. This means that God is constantly leaving himself to give himself to and to exist in Another. Each person of the Trinity exists in relationship toward Another. God is Father in Relationship to the Son. The Son exists and lives only in and for the Father, to whom he gives himself entirely. Their mutual love expresses itself in a procession of Personified love, the Holy Spirit. To pray in the heart is to experience this immense circulation of love among the Persons within the divine family, drawing us into that same community of love.[5]

[4.] Writings from *The Philokalia of the Heart*, E. Kaloubovsky and G. E. H. Palmer (trs), London, Faber and Faber, 1951, p. 84. Cited by Moloney, *Invaded by God*, p. 19.

[5.] Moloney, *Invaded by God*, pp. 19–20.

St Paul described this experience as 'seeing' the mysteries or secrets of God being made known in Christ, that in and through him we might become heirs of eternal life. While this theme forms the opening chapter of Ephesians, it is fundamental to Paul's understanding of the Christian life. He who is the image of the invisible God, declares that we can know by way of experiencing something of the inner life he lives with the Father in the Holy Spirit. For 'eternal life is this, to know you, the only true God and Jesus Christ whom you have sent'(John 17:3). Baptised into his death and resurrection and fed by the Eucharistic Bread that makes us incorporate in him in the mystical body of Christ Our Lord, means that we live and dwell in him and he in us in the Holy Spirit. Through the Holy Spirit we know that divine life in an experience of the Presence of Persons. True Christianity is the Presence of Persons, the divine presence, the oneness of God in a Trinity of Persons, to be experienced and known now, for they will come and make their home with anyone who loves the Son and keeps his Word.

> The doctrine of the Trinity is not only what makes Christianity uniquely different from all other religions, but it is a reality that effects the fulfilment of our very being as human persons. Christology and all other dogmas, Liturgy and the sacraments, preaching the Gospel and developing the Christian life of Christ-like virtues, all have their meaning and subordination to the central teaching of the Trinity.[6]

An ecclesial experience

Our experience of the divine presence can never be an individualistic experience of the flight of the alone to the Alone. It is given concretely in the sacramental life of the Church. Our experience of God and our knowledge of him are mediated through our membership of this covenant community. As the Godhead is a Trinitarian community in the oneness of divine nature, we too are

6. Moloney, *Invaded by God*, p. 21.

'members one of another' in that same community, in the divine humanity of the God-man Christ communicated by the grace of God's Spirit. It is man's 'original' humanity made perfect by God. It is the only humanity we know, the only one, which exists; restored, resurrected, renewed, recreated. It is the humanity of Christ in which people are born on the day of their baptism, confirmation, and first participation in the Eucharist.

Jesus is the real ladder bridging earth and heaven, the Son of Man who joins 'the seen to the unseen, God and Man in one'. Through him our spirits rise to God, through him God's Spirit comes down upon us.

> In the Church of Christ human persons enter paradise and become partakers of the nature of the Holy Trinity. The Church's Eucharistic sacrifice is the all-embracing act of her self-realization as a sacramental community. As such, the Eucharist is the expression of the very substance of the Church as salvation itself. The Church is salvation because her very being is communion with God, and with all things in Him, 'things in heaven and things on earth'. In the Church human beings participate in the divine liturgy of the Trinity, the 'common action' of the three divine persons: Father, Son and Holy Spirit. (The word liturgy means common action). They join the celestial liturgy of the angels, entering into the ceaseless singing of the thrice-holy hymn to the Creator. They join in the cosmic liturgy, participating with the heavens and the earth and all of the creatures in 'blessing the Lord' and 'proclaiming the glory of God.' They enter a reality incomparably more fearful and glorious than even that 'terrifying sight' upon the mountaintop, which caused the ancient Moses to 'tremble with fear'.[7]

The reality of the Church is nothing less than God with man and man with God, in the perfect community of truth and love, in the perfect unity of being and life, in the perfect liberty of the life-giving Trinity.

> The Church is the new creation. She is the union of many persons graced by God's Spirit, to be Christ's Body and his bride. She is the experience here and now in this age, in time

---

[7.] Thomas Hopko, *All the Fulness of God*, New York, SVS Press, 1982, p. 38.

and in space, of the kingdom of God not of this world, the new heaven and the new earth of the new man in the new Jerusalem foretold by the prophets, fulfilled in the Messiah and his Spirit, and beheld in the mystic vision of the Apocalypse as the very life of the world to come. And she is not only total newness; she is total fullness as well: the participation in the humanity of Jesus, the incarnate Word, in whom dwells the whole 'fullness of the deity bodily' and in whom human beings come to the 'fullness of life' (Col. 2:9). For 'of his fullness have we all received grace upon grace' (John 1:16). She is the Church which is Christ's body and his bride, 'the fullness of him who fills all In all' (Ephesians 1:23).[8]

The font is the grave in which we die with Christ, but also the womb, in whose waters we are reconstituted for rebirth into the new life of the divine humanity of the God-Man Christ. Sealed by the Holy Spirit in Confirmation, we are made capable of living the life of God into which we are born in Baptism, after which we are led to partake of the Bread of Life around the Eucharistic table. It is a present experience. The Eucharist becomes the manifestation of this new life. It is the sacrament of Christ's coming and presence. Here on the Lord's Day, which is also called the first day of the New Creation, rooted in the resurrection of Christ, Christ the Light and Life of men, comes into the midst of his own at the weekly Easter.

The First Day is also the Eighth and becomes the symbol for eternity. Eternity is the age in which we now live, because to partake of the life of God is to participate in that which is beyond time. It is to participate in life, which is everlasting. So the Eighth Day becomes the figure of life everlasting, the symbol of this present time of eternity in which we now live because of Christ. Therefore it is the day without evening, the last day, because no other day can follow eternity. So the Eucharist makes the Church what she is, witness and participant of the presence in the world of the New Life of the Kingdom. Here we assemble to hear his Word, as we eat and drink at his table in his Kingdom, that Christ may fill all things with himself. This presence of the 'now' in the 'not yet' is what relates the

---

8. Hopko, *All the Fulness of God*, pp. 34-5.

Church to the world and gives her the victory that overcomes the world.

In the best sense of the word the Church is a realm of grace, a communion of persons living in the life that Christ shares with the Father in the Holy Spirit, the New Life and knowledge of God in his Kingdom. The *Lex credendi*, the rule of faith, is something given and experienced in the *Lex orandi*, the rule of prayer and worship. They are organically related to one another and cannot be separated without damage to both. It is what Michael Ramsey describes as doing theology to the sound of church bells, because the Liturgy is the place where our knowledge of God is given in the realm of faith as experience, the *sui generis* experience of the Church.

Icon of God

This knowledge of God, given in the realm of faith as experience, the corporate experience of the Church, implies knowing God in the true sense of the root meaning of 'know', which is to become one with the object of knowing. To know God in this sense is to rest in God, which St Augustine said is the end of man. 'You have made us for yourself, O Lord, and our heart can never rest, until it rests in you.' To be truly human, man must live in God and God in him, to which the Incarnation testifies. His life if it is to be fully human, is to be a practical, dynamic and concrete way of life in God. 'The glory of God is a living man, and the life of man is the vision of God', is the way St Irenaeus expressed it. The nature of man derives from spiritual vision, spiritual understanding, and is fused, though not confused with this spiritual content. Man is not a self-contained whole complete in himself. His full nature cannot be understood, except within the context of a communion of life with God in which he partakes of the divine nature, becomes the likeness of the image in which he is made. As already stated St Athanasius described it in these words, 'God became man in order that man might become God.' Humanity is to be fused though not confused with divinity. Man's destiny is to be divinised.

The worship of God alone is the life in which man comes to himself and achieves his destiny.

In this sense Man is to be an icon of God, and his 'full nature cannot be understood unless he is seen in relationship to the organic whole of the spiritual reality of which he forms a part. He is to live within a particular framework of belief and worship, in order that he might manifest, convey, and give support to the spiritual facts undergirding human existence and underlying the liturgical drama of the Eucharist. The Liturgy conveys the Gospel lifestyle in a Eucharistic shape that man may participate in it and manifest it. As the destiny of Jesus was bound up with the Eucharistic Bread, so too is man's. The Bread, which is taken, blessed, broken and given, is Jesus says, 'My Life', but also, 'This is your Life, this is what Life is all about'. Our identity and destiny are also bound up with that piece of bread, the Bread of Life, which is nourished from 'My food, which is to do the will of Him who sent me'. To be the Body of Christ means too that we must be taken, consecrated, broken and given, distributed, that each of us may become a means of grace, a vehicle of the divine life, a Eucharistic presence. What happens in the Eucharist must happen in us.

The Bread, which comes down from heaven is for us the nourishment and sacrament of Life, because such Life gives us the capacity to give visible shape to death, suffering, love, fear and grief. It gives us the power to take these things into ourselves, to draw them back into life, that they may be reshaped by Life itself. Life for man is more than survival. Are we not the Easter people? Like Ezekiel before us we know that these dry bones can live again, for the vision in which we live is the reality of the Resurrection, the only event in history, which is ultimate.

The Eucharist is to convey this experience of reality as the consummation of Incarnation and Transfiguration, the two poles of the Christian scheme of salvation. For as the Incarnation signifies the entry of Spirit into matter, into human and natural existence, so the Transfiguration signifies the consequence of this, the sanctification or divinisation of human and natural existence. The Eucharist imitates and repeats this scheme. 'God became man, that man might become God', expresses what this scheme of salvation is, and the Eucharist becomes the vehicle of this divine life, saving life, continuing through time the redemptive activity of Christ, an image of the reality of Christ with the capacity to bring about man's salvation.

The nature of this image is something more than a mere indication of something else. By virtue of sharing in the nature of the object of which it is an image, there is an interpenetration of the one in the other, a physical fusion, though again not confusion. Hence, to know the image instantly makes one aware of the object it reveals, effecting rather than merely indicating what it signifies; and thereby, to the extent that one is open and receptive to its influence, one actually experiences the life which it mysteriously mirrors and enshrines. The Eucharist is such an image of the divine life which is 'the Light of men' and 'was made flesh'. To those who open themselves to this reality of divine life and move towards it, receiving Him and believing in His name, He will give power to become children of God, 'born not of blood, nor of the will of the flesh, nor of the will of man but of God' (John 1:12–13). The Eucharist communicates to us this 'divine life', so that we become in our turn a centre of power, an incarnation of the spiritual energy of God. We participate in and partake of the Life that is more than human and thereby we are able to induce in others a consciousness of this more than human life, which we embody. Eucharistic man testifies therefore to the basic realities of the Christian Faith, to the reality of the divine penetration in the human and natural world, and to the reality of sanctification, which results from this.

As an icon, Eucharistic man is not to be a mere imitation or copy of humanist models of self-realisation and self-fulfilment. He is to convey a picture of the divine world order, a picture of how things are in their true state, how things are in the 'eyes of God', and not as they appear to us from our limited point of view. This will only become possible in so far as man lives in and from the Spirit of God. For the likeness of God in man is a spiritual likeness and exists only in the Spirit. Such knowledge comes through personal participation in the object of our knowing, a love-knowledge, which cannot come by way of detached empirical observation, but only through an inward merging and identity with it. Man has to grow into that 'oneing with God', to use Julian's phrase, becoming one with whom he represents. In our quiet waiting upon God our vision widens, until we can see things from 'God's point of view'. We grow into a mental capacity able to accept that which we are to express, until it lives in us with its own inherent vitality. Our life becomes one of unceasing renewal and growth through an interior disciplined living in the Spirit, in whom are recreated the spiritual realities of which man is to be the icon.[9]

This takes us beyond the superficialities of a mere self-expression, which has become dominant today in the modern deification of self-realisation and self-fulfilment that calls itself 'modern spirituality'. As an icon of God, we cannot be concerned with expressing ourselves in this superficial sense, for as Merton says we will only end up impersonating a shadow. Our concern must be with revealing those forms of divine energy and life, not in any contrived sense, but which issue spontaneously from our own experience of them. Our primary concern must be, to avoid being moved by anything less than that centre of motivation and love that we have discovered at the heart of these forms of divine energy and life. What will then find expression in us will be that ultimate love, freedom, and spontaneity which lies at the heart of our own being as of all other being.

Understanding human nature in this sense, not only gives us a means of presenting doctrine in a living way, it also gives us a means for bringing about its spiritual realization. For doctrine is not theory, but living realities in which we live, and through which we receive the vision in which to see and understand what life is. The essence of the Christian Greed is not mere thought, but experience, the experience and awareness of 'the grace, love, fellowship and joy of "God with us"'. The thought is but one

---

9. Middleton, *Towards a Renewed Priesthood*, pp. 129–31. I have repeated the material here because of its relevance to the life of prayer.

mode of expressing that experience, and only by entering into the experience will that expression of doctrine reveal its secrets in a living way. It has to be lived before it can be properly thought about. Living comes before thinking and thought must never be confused as existence. So too we must first learn how to worship before we can properly know how to inquire. Hence, doxology becomes the best form of communication for doctrine, the type of insistent prayer that takes the Kingdom by force. Christian thought is never the mere product of the mind, and like life is much larger than logic.

As icons of God, we are to be a living illustration of the Christian Creed, presenting theology existentially, as we integrate in our being a doctrine of Creation, Incarnation, Crucifixion, Resurrection and Transfiguration. We are to be a living image of the Christian scheme of salvation, instructing by illustration the dogmatic truths of the Faith 'once delivered to the saints'. Our mission is to help make us conscious of the intellectual framework within which the Christian mystery unfolds, as we point away from ourselves towards that of which we are the image. The way of conversion for the modern mind will not be through confrontation in argument, or by accommodation of the Christian mystery to the modern mind's mode of understanding. The way in will be through the heart. Only when the heart is touched by these divine realities will the 'myths' of the modern mind be exploded.

The process of appropriation, is a process that goes on in a human milieu, a communion of persons tied by a presence and called to be witnesses to this presence, to be bearers of an awareness of the grace, love, fellowship, and joy of 'God with us' (Matt. 1:23). This interpretation involves a person-to-person relationship. We cannot institutionalise the world into God's Kingdom, and we will not fulfil our witness except by intimate relationship with ordinary people. In this perspective, the divine revelation has to be expressed not merely as a historical and social element of the past, but rather as the Incarnate Word in the Church of the present. It is not simply a law to be followed, a set of facts to be believed, or even a history to be accepted. It is all of this, but it is also more: it is a relationship to be received and experienced (1 Cor. 2:12–16). Some may dismiss this as being obscure mysticism, but there is in it something more than abstract emotionalism. It is a Christ-mysticism, which, as such, is a 'bound' mysticism, bound in history to the event of the Incarnation, which is being constantly renewed in the life of the Church and expressed in its inner life of prayer, as a sacrifice of praise offered on behalf of the whole universe,

Christian Faith is more than mere ideology, it is a matter of growing in the Spirit which prevents such ideas and beliefs from becoming static. Doctrine is living reality, states of power within us as well as within the universe. We are to visibly manifest or image these states. Being in communion with the life of what we see and touch, we become such centres of power within ourselves, an incarnation of the spiritual energy of God. This enables us to communicate to others, to induce in them a consciousness of this power and presence of divinity, in the language of a life that manifests an ever-increasing measure of discretion and discernment. Expressing through the beauty of a lifestyle that is rooted in a communion of life not our own, as an icon we manifest the true purpose of the human person, drawing others by the power of the life in which we live, to a realisation of that purpose. Hence they in their turn begin to experience, know and understand, something of the reality in which we live and which we seek to express.

Ultimately, as an icon, redeemed and regenerated, our purpose is to so affect people whom we meet that they may be transformed by the vision they see. For it is a vision of wholeness that holds together in a single vision, eternity and time, spirit and matter, the divine and the human. Each is an aspect of that one Reality, the Light which is the Life of men in which all things live and move and have their being, and which is manifested supremely in the saints.

> Then like them we'll brightly shine,
> With their Light, the Life divine;
> Life that is the Truth, the Way,
> In God's presence ev'ry day.

12

Transfiguration

I do not say that all is accomplished at once as soon as we attain this conscious communion with God. This is only the foundation laid for the next stage, for a new chapter in our Christian life. From now on the transfiguration or spiritualization of soul and body will begin as we share increasingly in the spirit of life that is in Jesus Christ. Having mastered himself, man will begin to instil into himself all that is true, holy, and pure, and to drive out all that is false, sinful and corporeal.

Bishop Theophan

My hope is similar in spirit to the way in which Thomas Merton wrote in the Preface to the Japanese edition *The Seventh Storey Mountain*. The words I have written, I hope will speak to you in a particular way that will not be confined to the words of a priest, who is also a preacher, a pastor, and a theologian. My hope is that they may speak to you in some way as your own self. One cannot tell where this will lead or what it will mean. If in your reading you have been listening and have heard what these words mean, then a language may well have been communicated, which may in some part have come through, though not merely from, the author of this book. This language will have come from the One who lives and speaks in us both, spontaneously communicating for all to hear, 'everyone in his own language, the wonderful things God has done'. If this happens, then what has been written will be more than a mere sharing of words and ideas, of dreams and visions, but a sharing of life so that we can say 'It is good Lord for us to be here'.

To pray is to grow into an ever-increasing sharing of Life with God, an ever-increasing sharing of the divine life that the Father lives with His Son in the Holy Spirit, and so to see the life of prayer as a re-enactment of the Transfiguration is not to project a fantasy. What the reality of the Transfiguration professes, is what we experience in prayer over a long gradual process of being transfigured in Christ, as we partake of the divine nature. It is to let the self, the real and true self, be transformed and transfigured in the milieu of divine life that God invites us to share in him. Prayer and life become integrated as we bring the real and total situation of personal and communal life in which we participate, into the larger context of the divine milieu giving it a new meaning.

There will always be the temptation to return into the security of life's earlier experience, or to escape into pseudo-reality. But the implication of the Transfiguration means taking the total, real, and actual circumstances of life as they are being lived and experienced, into the glory that will give meaning to it all. The experience will not be in terms of some other world, but of life as it is, renewed and transformed in Christ, made into the knowledge of and communion with God and His Kingdom. It is an experience radically new because it is not 'of this world', but whose gift and presence, continuity and fulfilment in this world is the Church. Therefore it is not a private and subjective individual religious experience. As stated previously, it is the unique and *sui generis* experience of the Church, the experience of the Church as new reality, new creation, new life, the Christ-life in which creation and life are renewed and transformed in Him.

Each of us in Baptism becomes a seed implanted into this new reality, that we might grow to full maturity as a child of God. We are endowed with the power of the Trinitarian life, whereby God's interior activity in us and our cooperation with him, lead us into the measure of the stature of the fullness of Christ. This growth is a movement in assimilating love, which prayer deepens, as it leads us into a long gradual process of transfiguration in Christ. As prayer and life are integrated and we begin to respond to the re-integration of our inner being, so we become more sensitive to God's dynamic presence breathing his life into us, that faith may be deepened and ourselves purified. To use again that phrase of St Irenaeus, 'the two hands of God, Jesus Christ and the Holy Spirit are continuously touching the soul'. This loving presence of God penetrates our whole being, creating, redeeming, and transforming us into a greater oneness with Christ. 'The Light which is the Life of men' is experienced as a transfiguring power. In this experience of the fullness of Baptism we are moving out from the darkness of self-centredness into the light of God's presence.

To say then, 'It is good Lord for us to be here', is to echo what the three friends of Jesus expressed on the mountain of Transfiguration. In a sense we have been climbing a mountain and the discipline of Christian life and prayer that assists such a climb is never easy. Though the climb may at times be difficult, the conviction of the Presence that Our Lord is leading us has always been certain. He is concerned to lead us into following him that we might become more conscious of an ontological life of Christ living in us through the sanctifying life of the Holy Spirit. To follow him that we might worship him and find that he is always the Way, the Truth and the Life.

His purpose in leading us, is to give us in this workaday world of Transfiguration, a glimpse of the Father to whom He leads us. He has no desire for self-glorification because, 'If I glorify myself, my glory is nothing'. Moses and Elijah bear witness not only to this same divine presence of the Father, but also to the Son in whom their witness finds its fulfilment. A ministry of Word and Sacrament has handed on to us 'the faith which was once delivered to the saints', in which Our Lord manifests Himself to us. What is foretold in Scripture, is in the Eucharist fulfilled before our eyes.

> That which was from the beginning which we have heard, which we have seen with our eyes, which we have looked upon and touched with our hands concerning the Word of Life ... the Life was made manifest and we saw it and testify to it and proclaim it to you, the eternal life which was with the Father and has been made manifest to us. (1 John, I. i)

In Scripture and Liturgy wedded together, we have been caught up in the wonderful works of God in order to share in them personally. Here God has come to us in his sanctifying power. 'Truly the Lord is in this place, Bethel, House of God, Bethlehem, House of Bread, Emmanuel, God with us', Jesus, Risen, Ascended, Glorified. We have come in a spirit of thanksgiving, penitence and love and been glad that we had come and with ease could say.

> It is good Lord for us to be here
> Thy beauty to behold,
> Where Moses and Elijah stand
> Thy messengers of old.

The ancient symbol of God's Presence, the overshadowing cloud, that conviction of God's Presence, has been as certain for us as it was for Mary when overshadowed at her Annunciation. The same still small voice of divine command can become as real for us as for those servants at the wedding in Cana, when we are told too, to listen and obey, to do whatever the Son commands. If anything is to happen it will need response, the 'So be it' of Mary, 'the mine not thine' of the Son, the doing of whatever He says because it is the Father's will.

For what we experience in prayer is authentically from God, the vision of a light shining, which is not of this world, from the maker of heaven and earth uniting us to himself and holding us in the embrace of his love. Such authentic experience, the 'tasting' of the divine life and presence opens us to God in all life, in all creatures, in the world around us as we discover him to be the source of all life, joy, light and hope. Not surprisingly the world around us takes on a new meaning as a transfiguring process begins to affect our vision of the world. This sense of God awakens us to a new kind of awareness in Christ, created in Him, redeemed by Him, to be transformed, transfigured and glorified in and with Him. All life takes on a new meaning. To use William Blake's phrase, 'The doors of perception are opened'. We realise that the world has not changed, but that our vision of it has been altered. God's Presence was always there but we were blinded to his

Light. Now the blind receive their sight and in consequence the darkness is lifted so that everything is suffused
in light.

> ... the real sense of our own existence, which is normally
> veiled and distorted by the routine distractions of an alien-
> ated life, is now revealed in a central intuition. What was lost
> and dispersed in the relative meaninglessness and triviality of
> purposeless behaviour (living like a machine, pushed around
> by impulsions and suggestions from others), is brought
> together in a fully conscious integrated significance. This
> peculiar brilliant focus is, according to the Christian Tradi-
> tion, the work of love and the Holy Spirit. This 'loving knowl-
> edge', which sees everything transfigured in God, coming
> from God and working for God's creative and redemptive
> love and tending to fulfilment in the glory of God, is a
> contemplative knowledge, a fruit of living and realizing faith,
> a gift of the Spirit.[1]

In this way of prayerful living, the way to life is through
death, an existential disposing of ourselves in the way of
Pascha Christi, so that the death and resurrection of
Christ takes hold on one's life and transforms it. Such
prayer is not a way of doing something, but a way of
becoming someone, becoming oneself, one's real self,
created by God, redeemed by the Son that makes us a
temple of the Holy Spirit.

It is one thing to have such vision, but quite another to
live in the light of it in obedience to its command. There
comes with certain inevitability the moment when this
vision has to inform and transform the features of life's
reality in the workaday world. We must come down from
the mountaintop and be immersed in life on the plain.
These features of life are transient and will continue to
change over the years, bringing sorrow as well as joy,
suffering as well as health and happiness, fulfilment and
disappointment, success and failure. These are the changing scenes of life in which many will struggle from sorrow
into joy in the dawning of a new day.

[1.] Thomas Merton, *Contemplation in a World of Action*, New York,
Doubleday Image Book, 1973, p. 176.

We cannot linger in the glory of the mountain vision with our backs turned on what is irksome in the life of our workaday world, the backyard of our lives. The irksomeness of life, the conflicts and burdens, joys and sorrows, successes and failures, must be carried into that vision so that they can be transfigured with us. Our frustrations and disappointments with their sufferings and conflicts, the 'thorns in the flesh', have to be taken into that supernatural context. When we do this we will find that it makes all the difference to the way in which we live through them and even look at them. They do not magically go away, the memory of them continues and the pain may continue to hurt, but in that environment of divine life and love in which the Father lives with Jesus our crucified and glorious Lord in the Holy Spirit, they will be transfigured. As the experience brings his glory right into our backyard so it lights up the treasure buried there, as it brings new life, light, joy and hope in the peace of his Presence that gives this 'irksomeness' new meaning.

If asked to sum up what I have written, this is how I would describe it. My aim has not been to bring you some technique to solve your problems, but to bring you to Jesus, the Author and Finisher of our Faith, that you may find in Him the science of the saints. For the ministry I have is not my own but his. '... we preach not ourselves, but Christ Jesus as Lord and ourselves as your servants for Christ's sake'. He it is who will continue the good work begun in you and who is the foundation upon which everything else must be built. It will be in your heart that the record of these words will be written and that is why 'It is good Lord for us to be here'.

Part Two

Some Practical Suggestions

1. Aids to Self-Examination

At the end of the day it is right that with God we should review it or examine what has happened by posing certain questions. Therefore in quietness and stillness ask the Holy Spirit to help. Use these words in which to phrase your prayer.

> Holy Spirit,
> Help me to see where I have been wrong,
> in thought, word and deed,
> the good I have omitted and the sins committed.
> In the light of the Father's presence in our Saviour
> Jesus Christ,
> show me the truth about myself.
> Give me strength to accept it,
> Grace to amend what is wrong
> and resolution to strive for the likeness of God in
> all that I think and do.

Self-examination may be posed in the form of a prayer

The following prayer comes from *My God My Glory* by E. Milner-White.

> Help me, O Holy Spirit, to search and question myself
> and honestly to answer:
> Am I single-minded in seeking my God?
> in serving him? even in praying to him?
> Do I put God first in deed? in intention?
> or even in desire? in hope?

What reserves do I always maintain against him?
  what other loves cling to?
Is not self-regard my prevailing motive,
  secret, silent, undetectable, insatiable?
Where do I serve self in daily conduct
  when I should be serving others?
  when I should be serving God?
Do I obey self even in the most inward spiritual things
  in the exercise of holy ministries ?
    even in the holiest place ?

  Search me thyself, O God
    seek the grounds of my heart;
Look well if there be any way of wickedness in me,
    any subservience to mine ease,
    any hungering and playing for mine own honour.
Help, O help me slay my self-regard,
    the foe that is in myself and of myself,
    and to want to slay it.
O Saviour of the world, who by thy Cross and precious
Blood hast redeemed me
save and help me, I humbly beseech thee, O Lord.[1]

Using the Beatitudes: Matthew 5:1–12

Do I know and acknowledge my need of God?

Am I regular and consistent in worshipping God and receiving Holy Communion, in the time I give to prayer and listening to God, in reading the Bible?

Do I feel genuine sorrow and concern at the ills and suffering in today's world?

Do I try to alleviate it by the way I think, what I say and what I do? Or am I too selfishly concerned for my own comfort and self-preservation? What must I give?

---

[1] E., Milner-White, *My God and My Glory*, London, SPCK, 1956, p. 23.

Am I possessed of a gentle spirit?

Do I try to live in a spirit of true Christian humility? Or do I easily become jealous, envious and bitter when someone receives what I want?

Am I always concerned to see that right prevails?

Am I easily swayed to seeking my own advantage or someone else's advantage irrespective of whether it is right? Is political opportunity rather than what is right the motivation behind how I live, in the family and home, at work or in the Church? Am I always ready to thwart those who threaten my ambition rather than admit when they are right? Is my concern always to undermine such people?

Am I a merciful person?

Am I a forgiving person or one who takes offence quickly and thereby easily harbour malice? Am I sensitive to the failings, needs and problems of others? Do I use them to magnify myself? How helpful am I to the need of someone I may not like?

How pure is my heart?

What motives determine how I think and live? Is it lust, pride, envy, greed, jealousy, covetousness, inferiority, malice? Am I dishonest? Am I unwilling to trust God and others? What are my besetting sins?

Or am I motivated by the fruits of the Spirit, love, joy, peace, kindness, long-suffering?

Am I a peacemaker?

Do I try to understand other people their reasons for thinking, acting and reacting in a particular way? Am I able to see things from another's point of view, or must it always be from my own? Do I always seek reconciliation where there are differences or do I glory in perpetuating division? Am I an aggressive person? If so what is my problem?

Am I prepared to suffer for what is right?

Am I prepared to suffer for matters of Christian principle? Or am I afraid of humiliation and ridicule? Am I a person of Christian integrity or do I always dodge the issue for fear of the consequences?

Using 1 Corinthians 13

Am I a person without love?
Am I patient?
Am I a kind person, without envy for anyone?
Is boastfulness a besetting sin?
Am I a person full of pride?
Am I conceited?
Do I indulge in rudeness?
How selfish am I?
Am I a person who is quick to take offence?
Do I harbour the wrongs people do to me?
Do I gloat over other people's failings?
Am I long-suffering?
Do I delight in the truth, even when it is about myself?
Are there limits to my faith and hope in God?
Are there limits to what I will endure for God?
Am I growing in my love for God and my faith in Him?

2. Acts of Confession

Use the prayers suggested in chapter 4. Two additional forms from E. Milner-White provide useful alternatives.

Confession

Forgive me, O Lord,
O Lord forgive me my sins,
    the sins of my youth,
    the sins of the present;
    the sins I laid upon myself in an ill pleasure,
    the sins I cast upon others in an ill-example;
    the sins which are manifest to all the world,
    the sins which I have laboured to hide from mine
acquaintance,
        from my own conscience,
        and even from my memory;
my crying sins and my whispering sins,
my ignorant sins and my wilful;
sins against my superiors, equals, servants,
        against my lovers and benefactors,
sins against myself, mine own body, my own soul;
sins against thee, O almighty Father, O merciful Son
        O blessed Spirit of God.
Forgive me, O Lord, forgive me all my sins;
Say to me, Son be of good comfort
        thy sins are forgiven thee
in the merits of thine Annointed,
        my Saviour Jesus Christ.[2]

---

[2] E. Milner-White, *My God and My Glory*, pp. 25, 28.

A PARVULIS LIBERA ME, DOMINE
Keep me, O Lord,
   from the little, the interfering, and the stupid;
from the infection of irritation and anger over nothings;
   Deliver and keep me, O my Lord.

from all promptings to decry the person or work of others;
from scorn, sarcasm, petty spite and whisperings behind
   the back; from the dishonest honesty of frankness
   meant to hurt;
   Deliver me, and keep me, O my Lord.

from hasty judgements, biased judgements, cruel
   judgements,
and all pleasure in them; from resentment
   over disapproval or reproof,
whether just or unjust;
   Deliver me, and keep me, O my Lord.

from all imposition of my own fads and idiosyncrasies
   upon others;
from self-justification, self-excusing and complacency;
   Deliver me, and keep me, O my Lord.

3. Ways into Adoration

Adoration is not an attitude that can be contrived. It must spring spontaneously from an ever-deepening love-knowledge of God. From such living experience of God there emerges an awareness of how uniquely important he is for our lives in the life-giving love He never ceases to have for us. In the prayer of Adoration we respond by acknowledging and expressing our recognition of God's never failing loving kindness towards us, which can only reveal to us how wonderful he is. Such response can be nothing less than awe, wonder and adoration, which are not passing sentiments, but the expression of a devoted life.

His love draws out our love, and like any lovers we find ourselves compelled to share with God our beloved what we feel about him. As we begin to feel in our hearts the thoughts of our minds we shall want to tell God how wonderful he is, praising and adoring Him for being just what he is. This will find expression in our own words, or in words, which we may have made our own from the language of Adoration in the prayer of others. That is one way into the prayer of Adoration.

Another way is to use the particular expressions in which others have articulated what we are gradually beginning to experience. Not only can such expressions draw out and articulate for us what that experience of prayer is, they can also give further impetus to such prayer, if we will be prepared to allow such expressions of adoration to lead us into the experience that inspired them. Here are some suggestions.

Adoration in Holy Scripture

In Exodus 18:10–12 we read of the experience of the Israelites being delivered from slavery in Egypt. It was a time of overwhelming wonder expressed to God. The father-in-law of Moses is overjoyed and the words of Jethro's response are an expression of adoration to God.

> Blessed be the Lord, who has delivered you out of the hands of the Egyptians and out of the hand of Pharaoh. Now I know that the Lord is greater than all gods ...

In 1 Kings 8:56–61, after finishing a dedication prayer on the completion of the Temple Solomon blesses all the assembly of Israel in a prayer of adoration to God.

> Blessed be the Lord who has given rest to his people Israel, according to all that he promised: not one word has failed of his good promise, which he uttered by Moses his servant. The Lord our God be with us, as he was with our fathers; may he not leave us or forsake us ... that all the peoples of the earth may know that the Lord is God; there is no other ...

Deuteronomy 32:3–4 expresses the adoration of Moses:

> For I will proclaim the name of the Lord ... Ascribe greatness to our God! The Rock, his work is perfect; for all his ways are justice. A God of faithfulness and without iniquity, just and right is he.

At the end of his suffering and near despair and after all his questioning of God Job finds himself caught up in the prayer of adoration.

> I know that thou canst do all things, and that no purpose of thine can be thwarted. Who is this that hides counsel without knowledge? Therefore I have uttered what I did not understand, things too wonderful for me, which I did not know. 'Hear, and I will speak; I will question you, and you declare to me' I had heard of thee by the hearing of the ear, but now my eye sees thee; therefore I despise myself, and repent in dust and ashes. (Job 42:2–6)

In the prayer of adoration, not only do we see God as He is, but we see ourslves as we truly are and this naturally leads us into the confession of our own unworthiness. This is Job's experience.

The Prophet Isaiah tells Israel to look up in adoration at what they see:

> The Lord is the everlasting God, the Creator of the ends of the earth. He does not faint nor grow weary his understanding is unsearchable. He gives power to the faint, And to him who has no might he increases strength ... but they who wait upon the Lord shall renew their strength ...
>
> (Isaiah 40:28–31)

In the New Testament there is St Paul's famous passage:

> For I am sure, that neither death, nor life, nor angels, nor principalities, nor powers, nor things present, nor things to come, nor powers, nor height, nor depth, nor anything else in all creation, will be able to separate us from the love of God in Christ Jesus our Lord. (Romans 8:38–9)

There is also the famous passage:

> Blessed be the God and Father of our Lord Jesus Christ. By his great mercy we have been born anew to a living hope through the resurrection of Jesus Christ from the dead, and to an inheritance which is imperishable, undefiled and unfading, kept in heaven for you, who by God's power are guarded through faith for a. salvation ready to be revealed in the last time. (1 Peter 1:3–5)

The Revelation of St John is full of spontaneous acts of adoration:

This cannot be an exhaustive list, but sufficient to help you recognise other such prayers in your own reading of Holy Scripture.

Adoration in the Psalms

The Psalter has been described as a most truly human prayer book for it expresses not only the heights of man's spiritual experience but also the depths to which man can sink in the darkness and despair that can beset him in his spiritual pilgrimage. Behind their words there may well be the weight of three thousand years of longing after God, and their words uttered many thousands of times more. Yet in making these words the vehicle in which to express our own heart's longing, they can live again with their original freshness. Furthermore, by a living identification with the reality of the prayer they express, the same Spirit who breathed in the original psalmist now breathes in us as we use the psalmist's words. They can echo our own heart's desire.

Ps. 8 has as its theme the greatness of man as crown and lord of all creation. This finds its fulfilment in Christ where we see man in Christ exalted to be Ruler of the universe. It is an Ascensiontide psalm expressing what the Liturgy contemplates, the power and authority given to Christ in heaven and earth.

Ps. 18:1–2 David expresses his joy and thanksgiving to God in being delivered from his enemies and especially Saul. It is the adoration of a victorious heart. Its appropriateness for our own prayer lies in its application to the overcoming of our spiritual enemies through the power of God in Christ.

Ps. 27:1–6 These words express a confident trust in the unfailing providence of God, in the face of all that would try to destroy us.

Ps. 36:5–9 The Psalm contrasts the wickedness of ungodliness with the faithfulness and loving-kindness of God. These particular verses tell us that our safety and satisfaction lie in the loving kindness of God to which there is no limit. Can this become the spontaneous response of our heart's prayer in the teeth of our own experience?

Ps. 63:1–8 Here is a morning prayer. The spirit of the Psalm breathes a sense of communion with God, which is what awakens a longing for his presence.

Ps. 66:1–8 Here there rings a strong sense of thanksgiving which gives way to adoration. Not only does it recall what God has done for Israel but also ' ... what he has done for my soul'. This can only give cause for adoration to the rejoicing heart.

Ps. 93 The kingly rule of God is the theme of this Psalm. This is as firm as a rock and will not be moved by the restless waves of the world's nations. Where God's presence is manifest, there is his house, therefore let us bow down and worship the King.

Ps. 95 is known as *The Venite*, and is a call to worship as it warns us against disobedience.

Ps. 100 These words are familiar. The whole world is called to unite in the worship of God.

Ps. 111 God shows us something of the kind of person He is by what He does. The supreme revelation of his character is given us in Christ Jesus. Its words can be used to give expression to our own praise and adoration for the glory, righteousness and the mercy of God that God has allowed us to see.

Ps. 135:1–3 These words are probably from Israel's liturgy in the second Temple, (cf. Ezra 3:10). God's preservation of his people warrants our praise and adoration in which we express the joy of our thankfulness. Our own creation, preservation and all the blessings of this life must be the primary sources impelling us to joyful and spontaneous adoration.

Ps. 147 Here Yahweh, the God of all Creation and the Restorer of Jerusalem is being thanked. It was probably part of the liturgical prayer in which Israel celebrated the dedication of the wall of Jerusalem after the return from exile (cf. Neh. 12:27ff). But God is also the architect and builder of the Church as well as the architect and builder of each one of us. For these things there is much to praise the Lord.

Ps. 148 Heaven and earth are called with Israel to the praise of God. All creation is called to adore and praise God.

Ps. 149 Exile in Babylon was a painful though chastening experience for Israel. Their restoration as a nation in their own land is a cause for rejoicing in Yahweh their King and God. It increases their confidence in God for the future in that with Him they will be saved from their enemies. Our spiritual pilgrimage brings us times when God requires us to reassess our identity, that He might lead us into a keener sense of vocation. As we emerge, maturer in faith, more confident in trust and hope, there is cause for rejoicing.

Ps. 150 This call to the universal praise of God is familiar. It is the prayer of doxology, an ascription of adoration.

Adoration in the Liturgy

The Gloria can be usefully incorporated into one's personal prayer, a use that can have only beneficial effects on the corporate prayer of the whole body.

Shorter pieces of the Eucharistic Liturgy such as, *Holy, Holy, Holy, Blessed is He who comes ... Blessing and Honour, Thanksgiving and praise ... Christ has died, Christ has risen, Christ will come again*, are appropriate for personal prayer.

Adoration in Hymnody

There are many such hymns that can be used in a personal way. A few are obvious:-
    O Worship the King; Praise to the Holiest; Praise my soul; Glorious things of Thee are Spoken

4. Planning Thanksgiving and Intercession

Expressing thankfulness to God is something that will arise spontaneously during the day as we notice things for which to be thankful. Similarly, we may be prompted to ask God's blessing on people and things as we read the newspapers or watch television or respond to the day's experiences. This is all part of the ongoing life of 'praying without ceasing' where we are and as we are prompted. However, as in life, so in prayer there is a need to plan, lest we forget to include within our ongoing thankfulness that for which we must be continually thankful. So too for intercession, a plan helps us to remember to pray for those who need our prayers.

Each person should work out his own plan and these suggestions are merely to help to this end.

Thanksgiving

There are various ways of planning such prayer, the variations being determined by the circumstances of people's lives. Some may find that a weekly plan is not possible and may opt to restrict such specific thanksgiving to a four-day scheme which operates from Monday to Thursday. Others may want to plan it over seven days, while others may want to have a specific thanksgiving for each day over a thirty-day period.

The Eucharistic Prayers of modern liturgies not only provide suggestions from which our personal thanksgiving can be guided, but words in which such thanksgiving can be expressed. Furthermore, it means that as we participate in the weekly Eucharist, our personal thanksgiving becomes Eucharistically rooted and centred. Such immersion of our own prayer in the communal prayer of the whole body not only enriches our own prayer but also the common prayer of the faithful with whom we participate.

A Four-Day Scheme using a Eucharistic Prayer

> It is indeed right,
> it is our duty and our joy,
> at all times and in all places
> to give you thanks and praise,
> holy Father, heavenly King,
> almighty and eternal God,
> through Jesus Christ your only Son our Lord.

Monday
For he is your living Word; through him you have created all things from the beginning, and formed us in your own image.

Creation, God's world, my creation. The family, parents, husband, wife, children. Our new creation in the living Christ.

Tuesday
Through him you have freed us from the slavery of sin, giving him to be born as man and to die upon the Cross; you raised him from the dead and exalted him to your right hand on high.

The Incarnation, Our Lord's life and teaching, God's Word in Holy Scripture, The Church of God.

Wednesday
The Death and Resurrection of Christ, life's blessings material and spiritual, colleagues at work, the ministry

of healing through priest, doctor, scientist, and nurse.

Thursday
Through him you have sent upon us your holy and life-giving Spirit, and made us a people for your own possession.

The gifts of Baptism and Confirmation, the Eucharist, unity and fellow Christians, the ministry and mission of the local church, the saints living and departed, the hope of glory.

Therefore with angels and archangels, and with all the company of heaven, we proclaim your great and glorious name, for ever praising you and saying:

Every day
Some particular blessing, something suffered for one's own good, e.g. hurt pride

> Holy, Holy, Holy Lord,
> God of power and might,
> heaven and earth are full of your glory.
> Hosanna in the highest.
>
> Blessed is He who comes in the name of
> the Lord. Hosanna in the highest.

These subjects for each of the four days may be taken one at a time during a period of a month. For example, the subject of Creation may be spread over the four Mondays of the month and similarly for each of the other days.

The whole prayer may be said each day putting in at the appropriate places the specific thanksgiving for each day. Let such expressions of thanksgiving be short and direct in a bidding form. It is as well not to get too cluttered up with too many words; quality not quantity is of the essence of prayer.

Here are some guidelines for a Weekly Plan, which again may form the basis from which a thirty-day scheme might emerge.

Sunday
Christ's resurrection, the Eucharist, my Communion, reading and proclamation of God's Word.

Monday
The Creator and His Creation, my own creation, the family; parents, husband, wife and children. Our new creation in the Risen Christ.

Tuesday
The Incarnation of Our Lord, material and spiritual blessings, people with whom I work, Our Lord's life and teaching.

Wednesday
The Church of God, my local church, the gift of the Holy Spirit, my Baptism and Confirmation.

Thursday
The Ascension, Our Lord's abiding presence, The Church's mission in the world, Unity and fellow Christians, Christ's ministry of healing through priest, doctor, nurse and scientist.

Friday
Christ's death on Calvary, Forgiveness of my sins, those who suffer in the spirit of Christ, all that destroys pride in me.

Saturday
The seed of eternal life in myself, the example of the saints living and departed, partaking of the divine nature, the joy and happiness of life in Christ and the hope of glory.

The Prayer of General Thanksgiving can be used and may also be adapted, its phrases being interspersed with specific points for thankfulness. Again the Eucharistic Prayers in the plethora of rites now available may be adapted and used. Another possibility is to write out one's own prayers of thanksgiving along similar lines.

Intercession

Again the planning of Intercession will be determined by the needs of individuals and the situations in which they live, and so there will be a variety of ways in which the plan of Intercession will take shape. If Monday to Thursday is one's *Days of Intercession*, then the Intercession from *ASB* or *Common Worship* of the Prayer for the Church Militant can become a useful aid. The words can be used and adapted to express the form of one's prayer, while each section will suggest a subject for each of the four days. Using one example:-

> Almighty God, our heavenly Father, you
> promised through your Son Jesus Christ to hear
> us when we pray in faith.

Monday
Strengthen our bishop and all your Church in the service of Christ; that those who confess your name may be united in your truth, live together in your love, and reveal your glory in the world.
The Church
Anglican, Roman, Orthodox, Free Churches. The Mission and Unity of the Church, Bishops and Clergy, Layworkers, Theological Colleges, Ordinands. The Growth of the Church in Prayerfulness and Faithfulness. Synods.

Tuesday
Bless and guide Elizabeth our Queen; give wisdom to all in authority; and direct this and every nation in the ways of justice and of peace; that men may honour one another, and seek the common good.
The World
The Queen and Nation, the Government and Parliament, the Judiciary, the Police. Other Nations and their Rulers, Peace, Sharing the World's Resources. Science and Education. Third World Needs.

Wednesday

Give grace to us, our families and friends, and to all our neighbours; that we may serve Christ in one another, and love as he loves us.

The Local Community

Local Government, Family Life, Employers and Employees, Unemployed, Trades Unions, The Rich and the Poor.

Thursday

Comfort and heal all those who suffer in body, mind, or spirit; give them courage and hope in their troubles, and bring them the joy of your salvation.

The Sick and Suffering

The sick, hospitals, chaplains, doctors, nurses, the hungry, the homeless, Christian Aid, Oxfam, NSPCC, the persecuted.

Friday

Hear us as we remember those who have died in the faith of Christ ... according to your promises grant us with them a share in your eternal kingdom.

Those who have died

Remember those who have died recently, those whose anniversary it is, relatives, friends, benefactors, those who have no-one to pray for them.

> ***Lord in your mercy***
> ***Hear my prayer.***

Such a petition can be used after each bidding within each section each day. Conclude your intercession each day with the words:

> ***Rejoicing in the fellowship of*** (mention names of patron saint, saints of day or week), ***all your saints, we commend ourselves and all Christian people to your unfailing love.***

> ***Merciful Father,***
> ***accept these prayers***
> ***for the sake of your Son***
> ***our Saviour Jesus Christ. Amen.***

A Monthly Plan

The subjects in this plan can be spread over the four Mondays of the month, and similarly for the other days.

A Weekly Plan

Sunday: **The Church of God** in Mission, Ministry and Unity, Anglican, Orthodox, Roman Catholic and Free Churches. Bishops, Clergy and Layworkers, Religious Communities, Theological Colleges and Ordinands, Synods. Growth in Faithfulness, Prayerfulness and Discipline.

Monday: **Nations**, States and World Leaders, The Queen and Nation, the Government and Parliament, Judges, Magistrates, Police, The Armed Forces, Agriculture, Industry and Commerce, Education, Science and the Arts.

Tuesday: **Relief Agencies** – Christian Aid, Oxfam, Bible Lands Society, N.S.P.C.C., Church of England Children's Society, Church Societies – Mother's Union, Diocesan Societies and Parochial Groups. Environmental and Peace Issues.

Wednesday: **The Anglican Communion**. The Missionary Societies, Christians under Persecution, International UNO, Amnesty International. World Peace, An End to International Terrorism, Issues Justice, Racism, Hunger and Disease.

Thursday: **The Local Church** in Ministry and Mission, The Diocese and Cathedral, Family Life, Parents and Children, The Homeless, Unemployed, Lonely People, Local Government.

Friday: **The Church's Ministry of healing,** Hospital Chaplains and Parish Priests, The Sick, Doctors, Nurses and Scientists, Hospitals, The Hungry, Bereaved, Handicapped, Those who Have Died, Relatives Ministering to the Dying, The Sick and Dying at Home. Enemies of Christ's Church, An End to Violence, Vandalism and Disorder, Those in Prison, the Prison Service.

Again appropriate sections of the Intercession from public worship rites may be used as the language in which to express such prayer. This plan can be spread over a thirty-day period. Use each day's suggestions and plan them over the four Sundays of the month, the four Mondays and so on. Again these suggestions are merely guidelines, neither limiting nor exhaustive. Some may want to use the plan as it is, others will want to catch the principle and spirit of it and compile their own. Some will have more time for intercession than others. The important point to bear in mind is not to allow oneself to be overburdened with quantity. The thirty-day plan or even sixty-day plan may well be the most appealing, giving something for intercession each day.

Other Forms of Intercession

On p. 166 of the *ASB*, *Alternative Forms of Intercession* are provided for use with the Eucharistic Rite. These can be adapted and used in a personal way. The Specific Intercessions for each day can be phrased in the form of biddings instead of using the words 'we' and 'us', use 'I' and 'me'. Alternatively use the Forms *in toto* as Acts of General Intercession.

The Litany Form can also be used in a personal way. The Litany is provided on p. 99 of the *ASB*. It is usefully divided into sections. Sections I and VI must always be used but selections can be made from appropriate parts as and when necessary. Alternatively, this too can be used as an Act of General Intercession.

The Litany Form can be adapted and used as a way of phrasing one's daily intercessions in one's own words. Here is an example:

For the Church of God

God the Father,
have mercy on me,
God the Son,
have mercy on me.
God the Holy Spirit,
have mercy on me.
Holy, blessed and glorious Trinity,
have mercy on me.

Hear my prayer, O Lord my God.
Hear me, good Lord.

As I pray for your Holy Catholic and Apostolic Church in all the world. Inspire, guide and renew it in the gifts of your Holy Spirit.
Hear me, good Lord.

Remember the Church in our own land. Renew it in mission, ministry and unity; remove what is evil, strengthen what is good; fill it with truth and love.
Hear me, good Lord.

Bless all Christian people and renew them in holiness. Strengthen all bishops, priests and deacons in their Ministry of Word and Sacrament. Quicken your whole Church in Worship, Witness and Service.
Hear me, good Lord.

Multiply our opportunities of service and give us grace to use them in unfailing steadfastness and devotion. Bless all who are called to particular ministries.
Hear me, good Lord.

Remember those in training for the sacred ministry. Guide them and their teachers in the way of truth and holiness, and turn the hearts of many to offer themselves for this work of ministry.
Hear me, good Lord.

Prosper the life, work and witness of our religious communities that they may be an authentic sign of your Kingdom. Call many more to the religious life.
Hear me, good Lord.

Prosper those being initiated into the Church's sacramental life. Increase in them your grace and keep them faithful.
Hear me, good Lord.

Prosper our children and young people and encourage those who teach and instruct them. Protect them from the temptations that would destroy their faith.
Hear me, good Lord.

Give me true repentance; forgive me, my sins of negligence and ignorance and my deliberate sins; and grant me the grace of your Holy Spirit to amend my life according to your holy word.

Holy God,
Holy and strong,
holy and immortal,
have mercy on me and hear my prayer.

The General Intercession may also be adapted for personal use.

Here is an example:

For the World

Hear my prayer O Lord for the world and its people;
> that your kingdom may be extended and your rule
> established.

Let me first pray for the Christian nations;
> that they may seek first the Kingdom of God
> and his righteousness,
> that they may seek peace among all men,
> and always what is just.

Let me pray for the United Nations Organisation;
> For the growth of peace, goodwill and unity,
> For the honouring of agreements,
> > a fairer distribution of the world's resources
> > especially of food and the necessities of life.
> For a concern to assist Third World development,
> > the condemnation of racism

I pray for all in positions of authority;
> Kings and Queens, Presidents and Ministers of State,
> that with their governments they may seek only your
> will,
> in the administration of justice and mercy,
> in their domestic and foreign policies
> in their exercise of liberty and law

Sum up this prayer and petition in the Lord's Prayer

Useful books:
Parish Prayers edited by Frank Colquhoun
Contemporary Parish Prayers by Frank Colquhoun
Leading Intercessions by Raymond Chapman
A Pastoral Prayer Book by Raymond Chapman

5. Keeping Useful Notebooks

A Notebook Anthology

This notebook is for one's own private collection of sayings and passages from the writings of other people. To collect them into such a notebook will ensure that one can keep re-reading them, meditate or ruminate on them. A collection can be built up over a period of time and if the book is kept near the bedside it can become bedtime reading. Passages can be collected from the Bible, Psalter, spiritual writers, perhaps even sermons. Just collect such striking passages as one's reading proceeds. If one wishes to index them so that they can be found quickly then in the back of the book an index might be kept, or a small indexed notebook kept for this purpose.

Such a book needs to be a hardback notebook 20cm × 25cm, with wide lines, preferably without a margin so that one can put in a margin of desired width. Number the page and use the margin for entering the title of the book, author and page number from which the passage comes.

Keeping such a notebook helps to clarify one's thinking and can be an invaluable aid to prayer.

A Notebook of Prayer

This is a different type of notebook. Its purpose is to assist in the planning of one's prayer and the informing of the memory about the particular concerns of one's prayer at particular times. As these may need to be changed and revised from time to time this notebook should be loose-leaf. It should not be too small, perhaps about 20cm × 15cm. The book will need to be divided into separate sections. A set of card dividers with an index leaf on the edge will be useful for this or a set of index strips from which a required index leaf of the required size can be cut and then stuck on the edge of the appropriate place of the particular page. On the index leaf will be written the appropriate title of each particular section of the book, for example Morning Prayers or Weekly or Monthly Intercessions. The required section of the book can be quickly turned.

A book like this will not take shape in one day but will need to be planned and built up over a period of time, as well as being subject to revision when the need arises. Here are some guidelines:

Daily Prayer

Using the suggestions already given, *A Form of Morning Prayer* and *A Form of Evening Prayer* can be written into this section. Use either an outline form which can be used in conjunction with the the Church's service books, indicating where the prayers will be found; or copy out in full the actual order of prayers in full. Then one will only have need to use the notebook.

There will be people and concerns for which one prays daily and so these will be included at some point, maybe for use at the end of Morning or Evening Prayers or at another time during the day, which could be before going to sleep at night. Also in this section a *Form of Self-Examination* can be written for daily use and with it a few alternative prayers in which to express one's Confession.

Prayers of Adoration

A selection of prayers of Adoration culled from the Bible, the Psalter, the Liturgy and the Hymn Book will provide a useful source for the daily expression of one's own adoration. Copy these into the book.

Plan for Thanksgiving

This may be planned over a four-day, seven-day or thirty-day period, the first two ways enumerating the subjects of thanksgiving under the days of the week. The third way will be done best by using the numbers 1–30, then each number can coincide with the date of the month. Again include in this section some prayers of thanksgiving in which one's own prayer can be expressed or references to which one can turn.

Plan of Intercession

Another section will be labelled Intercession and again will be planned over a four-day, seven-day or thirty-day cycle. The short-term cycles can use the days of the week into which subjects for Intercession can be divided. The long-term will use the numbering of 1–31 which will coincide with the date of the month.

Again collect and write into the notebook some forms which can be used in which to express one's prayer of Intercession. Various suggestions have already been made. These can be revised when the need arises.

Weekly Prayer

There may be particular people and matters for which one prays on a weekly cycle and which are outside one's normal plan of prayer but additional to it. Enumerate the days of the week and write in these matters for prayer.

Other People's Prayers

It is useful to have a section where one can copy in other people's prayers which we find attractive. Helpful pictures and devotional cards can also be included.

A Notebook of Private Devotion

This need not be a separate book but could form a section of one's *Notebook of Prayer*. The purpose of this exercise is to write one's own forms of prayer, of personal and private devotion. This is not a suggestion that one sits down and begins to compile prayers from the top of one's head. One must wait for that moment when such prayer is conceived in the heart and before it is born there may well be many inarticulate groanings. Nevertheless such an exercise can be a very useful aid to growth in prayer and our capacity to articulate such prayer will be proportionate to our growth. As we use the language of the Church's prayer as a vehicle in which to express our own heart's desire, not only do we grow in prayer but we familiarise ourselves with its language. The same experience results from the use of other people's prayers. Gradually the capacity to use that language in which to express our own personal experience of that 'communion with God', begins to emerge.

The phrasing of one's own private devotions will not be original. Rather will they be a patchwork of expressions woven together as they have been culled from the the Church's service books, the Bible and Psalter and from spiritual writers that have become part of one's reading. From such sources one is able to weave a pattern of daily occasional prayer, that can become the essence of one's life, the expression of the deepest aspirations of heart and mind, of one's whole being.

Here is an example of Morning Prayer:

ON WAKING

O Lord, in my waking, there dawns for me,
another day in which to be conscious of
Your Presence,
Your Indwelling.
Awaken me to inward sight of Yourself,
communion with You
and strength from You.
That my life today may sing the Lord's song,
in whatever strange land I find myself in.

So be it Lord, and in such prayer,
let my spirit dwell in You, this day,
all day.

WASHING AND DRESSING

Washing reminds me that in Baptism You
cleansed me in the Font's life-giving water.

Make me a clean heart O God, and renew a
right spirit within me, that today I may
continue to walk in the new life of the
Resurrection, and see all today's concerns
in the vision of eternity.

Let this washing be a blessing to my body,
a reminder to my soul, that body, mind and
soul may think and speak and do only what
is rightful in your sight.

As I clothe myself in the vestments of daily life,
may that life be a worthy offering
in worship, sacrifice and praise.

AN ASCRIPTION OF PRAISE

Glory to God the Father who created me,
Glory to God the Son who has redeemed me,
Glory to the Holy Spirit who sanctifies me.

To You Lord, my light and my salvation,
the strength of my life,
I give thanks;
for the rest of the past night,
the joy of a new day,
health and strength,
family and friends.
To you I look, to you I bow,
To you for help I call;

My life and Resurrection,
My hope, my Joy, my All.

A CONFESSION OF FAITH

I believe and trust in God the Father
Who made the world.
I believe and trust in His Son Jesus Christ
Who redeemed mankind.

I believe and trust in the Holy Spirit
Who sanctifies the people of God.

THE LORD'S PRAYER

COMMENDATION OF THE DAY

My Lord and My God, to you I commend this day.
Let my mind and heart dwell on:

whatever is true,
whatever is honest,
whatever is just,
whatever is pure,
whatever is lovely,
whatever is of good report

If there be any virtue, any praise,
let it be in the thinking and doing of these things.
So let me always sing praise to your Name, that
daily I may perform my vows.

A Form of Evening Prayer can be compiled along the same lines

The various parts of this night prayer would include the following:

Recollection	A prayer acknowledging God's presence, asking His guidance and inspiration, a humble spirit and sincerity of heart.
Confession	A prayer of General Confession that personalises for oneself 'the sins that so easily beset us'. Incorporated into this prayer would be a request for God's forgiveness.
An Ascription Of Praise	There will be many things in one's life for which to praise God. In our growing awareness of God we will want to sing the Lord's song because he has dealt so lovingly with us.
Intercession and Petition	A General Intercession for all sorts and conditions of people in their different situations. Incorporated into this will be a Petition for our own needs.
Commendation to God	A prayer commending oneself into the safekeeping of God.

6. Preparation and Thanksgiving for Holy Communion

Here are two prayers of Bishop Jeremy Taylor, an Anglican divine of the seventeenth century (1613–1667):

Preparation

Lord, let the Holy Sacrament of the Eucharist be to me a defence and shield, a nourishment and medicine, life and health, a means of sanctification and spiritual growth; that I, receiving the Body of my dearest Lord, may be one with his mystical Body, and of the same spirit, united with indissoluble bonds of a strong faith, and a never failing charity, that from this veil I may pass into the visions of eternal clarity, from eating thy Body to beholding thy face in the glories of thy everlasting Kingdom, O blessed and eternal Jesus.

Before Reception

Glory be to thee, O God our Father, who hast vouchsafed to make us at this time partakers of the Body and Blood of thy Holy Son. Keep us under the shadow of thy wings, defend us from all evil, and lead us by thy Holy Spirit of grace into all good: for thou who hast given thy Holy Son unto us, how shalt thou not with Him give us all things else? Blessed be the Name of our God for ever and ever.

Thanksgiving for Holy Communion

I will give you thanks O Lord with my whole heart and bow down before your holy temple:

> because of your faithfulness and loving kindness.
> At a time when I called to you you answered me
> and put new strength within my soul.
> In giving me Manna to eat, Food from heaven,
> you have fed me with the finest wheat flour
> of your own life, satisfying my hunger with
> good things,
> annointing me with the oil of gladness,
> the fruits of your Holy Spirit.
> Keep me in this mystical body of your Son,
> the blessed company of all faithful people.
> Assist me with your grace,
> that I may do all such good works
> as you have prepared for me to walk in;
> so that as I dwell in You and You dwell in me
> You may speak in me and through me
> at all times and in all places.

After Reception

Give unto me O God, and unto all that have communicated this day in the divine mysteries a portion of all the good prayers which are made in heaven and earth; the intercession of Our Lord and the supplication of all thy servants; and unite us in the bonds of common faith and a holy charity; that no interests or partialities, no sects or opinions may keep us any longer in darkness and division.

As one's prayer grows and increases with one's capacity for compiling such private devotions, so other prayers may emerge in one's notebook.

Suffering

Lord, Jesus Christ, who in the Bread of Life
Gave to us the nourishment and sacrament of Life;
enable me through this Life,
to give visible shape to death, suffering, love fear and
grief.
Give me power to take these things into myself,
To draw them back into myself,
Allowing them a renewed place in Life
That they my be reshaped by Life itself.

For New Opportunity

My Lord and My God,
Doors of opportunity have closed,
As bits of myself threatened me,
False fears overwhelmed me,
Lack of confidence defrauded me.
The opportunities are gone and the past is over,
Disillusionment and disappointment remain.
Yet I must move on,
Change my attitude of mind,
Let the past opportunities go,
Reach out anew in the present
And allow myself to be changed.
Lord help me to change,
That I might respond to new opportunities and not lose
any more.

There may well be a series of meditations for occasional
use, their themes being suggested by the events of Our
Lord's life.

(i) The Nativity
(ii) The Epiphany
(iii) The Baptism of Our Lord
(iv) His Temptations

(v) The Cross
(vi) The Resurrection.
(vii) The Ascension
(viii) The Coming of the Holy
Spirit.

Another section may well be a series of daily prayers, a different form for each day of the week planned in relation to Adoration, Confession, Thanksgiving, Supplication. Each day may lay a different stress on a particular aspect of prayer.

In Conclusion

Do realise that such a book cannot be compiled in a free evening. It will emerge and grow in proportion to one's capacity for prayer. The classic example of such a notebook of private devotion is *The Private Prayers of Bishop Lancelot Andrewes*. There are other classic examples in the history of Anglican devotion such as John Cosin's, William Laud's and Thomas Wilson's to name a few. Andrewes was an Anglican divine, born in 1555 who died as Bishop of Winchester in 1626. Published versions of these prayers are available and a look at them would be helpful because it is possible to adapt them to present needs.

7. Sources of Meditation and the Prayer of Quiet

The Readings for Sundays and Holy Days in the Church's Service Books

Here is a quarry of biblical material that can be followed sytematically as the Christian Year unfolds. Use the readings for meditation the week before the actual Sunday. In this way one's participation in the Ministry of the Word at the Eucharist on the Sunday following will be immensely enriched. The advantages of using such material from these books means that it is linked to the great doctrinal themes in the liturgical cycle of feasts. Bible, doctrine and liturgy are linked together in our personal prayer.

Readings for Weekdays

There is a regular cycle of Readings for Morning and Evening Prayer. Buy a lectionary each year before Advent. An Old Testament or New Testament reading may be chosen for each day from one of the four. Choose whatever is helpful. Again it has the added advantage of linking one's personal prayer with what the whole Church is doing and again bringing Bible, doctrine and liturgy together.

Using the Prophets, Gospels and Epistles

The prophets of the Old Testament can provide much food for thought that is profitable for meditation. Ruminate on what a particular prophet is saying.

The Gospels will be a primary source for meditation. Read a particular Gospel slowly and stopping where it seems thoughtful for meditation and prayer. Use them selectively, concentrating on the parables or the miracle stories, or the events of Our Lord's life.

The great doctrinal themes of the epistles are food for meditative pondering. Again select an epistle and move through it slowly until one is stopped for meditation and prayer.

The Prayer of Quiet

Those who want to quietly wait upon God, will find the Psalms an invaluable source of inspiration and strength. Become familiar with their language, and you will find particular phrases settling in your memory, as you enter into the experience of that essence of prayer the Psalm is articulating. Such phrases can be used as the expressions of your own prayer as you 'practise the presence of God', and begin praying without ceasing.

A way of becoming familiar with the Psalms is to say them each day on a regular basis. Again the Church's service books can be an invaluable aid. The lectionary gives regular cycles of psalmody with Psalms for each day. One may not be able to recite all the Psalms, but one may pick out one or two from the Psalms for the day and use them as a preface to one's prayer of quiet waiting upon God.

Useful Expressions from the Psalms

Your word is a lantern to my feet:
and a light to my path.

The Lord is my light and my salvation
Whom then shall I fear.

Create in me a clean heart O God
and renew a right spirit within me.

Help me O Lord my God:
and save me for your mercy's sake.

Many more such phrases for use in reducing one's prayer to the poverty of the single verse will be found in the Psalms. In the Gospels, sayings of Our Lord can be used:

Abide in me and I in you.

My peace I give to you.

From the Liturgy

Jesus, Lamb of God have mercy on me.

Lord have mercy,
Christ have mercy,
Lord have mercy.

Christ has died,
Christ is risen,
Christ will come again.

Single Words

Love, Peace, Truth, Joy, Light, Life, Wisdom.

8. Tips For Prayer Groups

Prayer groups begin to emerge when a sufficient number of people in a particular place share a common desire to discover more about prayer. It is a good way of finding mutual help and support in the way of prayer. In a parish or college setting one is frequently asked to advise on the setting-up and the running of such groups. So a few hints here may be found useful.

People will come with different expectations and so it is important at the outset to work out what the aim of the group is to be. It is expected that there will be a fluctuating fringe membership when those who come seeking from time to time, find that the group's purpose does not meet their expectations. This is no cause for anxiety. Similarly if the group is small do not become anxious. The primary objective is to mutually assist one another in the way of prayer, not to attract large numbers. There needs to be a sense of commitment about attendance at the meetings and no room for the casual floater who 'drops in' when there is nothing more important in the diary.

Of their nature these groups are not going to be very large, but even so, one hesitates to put an upper limit on the number in any one group; large and small groups can operate quite happily. Let the group decide how many it can carry. This may well be determined by other factors, such as the practical considerations of the place where the group meets.

Variety of Operation

There will be variations of the way in which groups operate depending on the aim of the group and the nature of how the agenda is organised in relation to time praying together, time for instruction and time for discussion.

Church or Chapel Centred

In the parish a group may be centred on the parish church. In a college it can be centred on the college chapel or the group may meet in a student's room. The frequency of meetings will be determined by the availability of time among its members, the week the fortnight or the month being the deciding factor of the cycle.

Neighbourhood Group

There may be the possibility of people in the same neighbourhood coming together into a group. Each member of the group may share the responsibility for providing the place of meeting, or it may be more convenient to meet in the same house on every occasion.

If there are a number of such groups, once they have decided upon the regular pattern of their meetings, they may then commit themselves to a three-monthly meeting where all the groups can come together in the parish church or the college chapel.

Leadership of Meetings

There is always hesitation because of a reluctance that the whole burden of responsibility for the group may fall to one person. This need not be so. The group will need someone to coordinate all the practicalities necessary for a group to function. Such a link person can delegate the sharing of such practicalities – the place and its

preparation for the meeting, the refreshments, the intro-
ducing of the theme and subject matter.

The leadership of the actual meeting itself in terms of its
theme and subject matter has a number of options. It can
be shared in rotation among those who are willing to be
responsible for it. One suitable person may have sole
responsibility. From time to time a person from outside
the group can be invited.

Timing of the Meetings

This will vary according to what the members want to do
as a group, and the availability of time among the
members. It is good to have it on a set day, a Monday or a
Tuesday or whatever, or on a particular day of the month
if a monthly meeting. Always have the same starting time
and the finishing time. Then people will always know how
much time they must allocate. Timetable for Prayer,
refreshments, study and discussion.

It is good to have a convenient time in the household or
college timetable that is least disruptive for those being
deprived of some of their accommodation. Practicalities
such as TV schedules and sports events are an important
consideration for many. Always start promptly and finish
punctually and do not linger or become distracted chat-
ting. A monthly meeting gives more opportunity for
discussion about matters of prayer, because people will be
more inclined to stay longer when the meeting is less
frequent.

Programming the Meeting

Initially this is the greatest difficulty for most groups.
Whatever the group it is essential that people arrive to
silence and then wait in silence for proceedings to begin.

Recollection

Begin punctually with a prayer recollecting the group in God's presence. Make it brief and direct and follow it by three or four minutes silence.

Liturgical Prayer

There is nothing more powerful than liturgical prayer for welding a group together into a prayerful fellowship. Whatever form is used will be determined by the timing of the meeting. If it meets in the morning then Mattins may be said in its Longer or Shorter versions or from *Celebrating Common Prayer*. If it is the afternoon or early evening then Evening Prayer can be used. Compline or Night Prayer as it is sometimes called, is another alternative and is a popular office among many lay people.

A Reading

Choose a suitable reading on Prayer from a book, maybe two, at the most three paragraphs. Anthologies of readings are good sources from which to select something useful. *The Art of Prayer* edited by Palmer and Kadloubovsky, is such a source book. Collections of *The Sayings of the Desert Fathers* are also helpful. So too are some of the Fairacres pamphlets.

Silent Prayer

After the reading members of the group can sit or kneel, as they find appropriate and remain in silent prayer for fifteen minutes. It is useful to give them a phrase for their careful and deliberate repetition during the silence.

Leader: *Hear some words of St Gregory of Sinai*
The gift which we received from Jesus Christ in holy baptism, is not destroyed, but only buried as a treasure in

the ground. Take care to unearth this treasure. It comes to
light and is revealed, through the continual invocation of
the Lord Jesus, or the unceasing remembrance of God,
which is one and the same thing.

> ***Our help is in the Name of the Lord***
> **All:** Who has made heaven and earth

> ***Jesus Christ, Son of God, have mercy on me.***
> **Silence**

Conclude with:

*The grace of Our Lord Jesus Christ, the love of God, and
the fellowship of the Holy Spirit be with us now and
always.*

A Candle

A useful aid to the focusing of the group's attention is the
presence of a lighted candle in house, student's room or
church.

Refreshments

After the devotional part of the programme it is helpful to
relax with a cup of tea and a biscuit, nothing more. Do not
let it become a competition about who can provide the
best refreshment.

Discussion

Then following the refreshment, or with it, can follow
discussion about matters of prayer. It is beneficial to bring
another mind into the group. This can be done by the
group reading together a book or a pamphlet and preparing for the meeting by doing their homework beforehand.

The book will not only provide interesting information about the life of prayer and answer many questions, it will stimulate a lot more and lead the group into all kinds of interesting discussion.

It is obvious that such a programme will occupy the best part of two hours. Weekly meetings and Neighbourhood Groups will not be able to give that amount of time. Therefore adapt it and tailor it to the needs of the situation. The weekly meeting may consider making one of their meetings an extended session of this kind, once every month or whatever.

Meetings for Leaders

If there are a number of groups in one place, a meeting for leaders from time to time might be helpful. Invite an outsider along who might give such help and let the leaders air their questions with such a person or merely with each other.

Quiet Days and Retreats

The groups might like to initiate extended periods of silence and prayer in the form of Quiet Evenings or Quiet Days and Retreats. Other members of the Christian community could be invited.

Conferences and Schools of Prayer

Once a year an annual conference might be held in the place where the groups operate. Speakers could be invited to speak on masters of the spiritual life, such as Julian of Norwich, Thomas Merton, The Desert Fathers etc. This can be done fairly cheaply and audiences invited from outside the immediate environment. Similarly a *School of Prayer* might be held from time to time. It is amazing what possibilities there are on our own doorstep.

Part Three
Appendices

Appendix 1

Retreats: Their Use and Abuse

Are there 57 Varieties?

Recently I browsed through the listing of APR *Retreats*.
The bold affirmation made in this journal is that so many
enigmatic variations on 'retreats' are provided in our
Retreat Houses. Nobody need be disappointed as there is
something to meet everyone's tastes and needs. This set
me thinking about what a retreat is and what it is not. Here
are my reflections.

The Aim of a Retreat

A retreat is the setting aside of a few days from our ordinary routine and the motive for doing this is to acknowledge God's claim upon us and that its fulfilment is our
true life. A retreat aims to deepen this sense of God's
claim, to give a soul a deepening awareness of God. The
conductor's aim is to help each retreatant to a realisation
of God-in-Himself, that he is before and beyond all that we
know, that he is eternal, holy and righteous, but also that
he is loving, near and tender. So the conductor will also
attempt to increase the realisation of God's will for each
retreatant, *God's will for me.*

What makes a Retreat is the surrendering of ourselves
wholly to the realisation of God for a few days. We put
away all else in order to wait upon him. It is this, together
with the method by which we are made ready and able to

hold to the one aim, that constitutes a retreat. So the word 'retreat' ought to be reserved for what is described and should not be applied loosely to refer to any casual Christian gathering. A retreatant must understand that he goes with the one aim defined here, and with the confidence that he will find all the various helps that he needs.

There is a threefold involvement in a retreat, the retreatant, the conductor, and the Holy Spirit. It is the Holy Spirit, not any technique of self-transcendence, which directs and overrules so as to give each retreatant the opportunity to find what he needs.

Withdrawal and Silence

A retreat is a deliberate choice to draw aside from our normal routine and interests, to wait on God until he speaks to us. Elijah heard God, not in the fire and thunder but in the silence of the still small voice. A retreat is basically withdrawal and silence while we wait for God to make himself known to us. Abraham, Jacob, St Paul, remained alone and apart with God to discover his will. Christ and his disciples went into a desert place when they were seeking God's will. This teaches us a further motive for retreat; that we owe it to God to withdraw at times in order to give him our undivided attention so as to serve him better.

Withdrawal and silence must be well used if the retreat is to be fruitful. In Word and Sacrament we focus and wait upon God because this is why we have come. We surrender ourselves in patience and trusting love, in devotion towards God. Gentle movements, a still tongue, a definite rhythm of thought guided by the routine of the day, help us to know his presence, and prepare our conscious and subconscious mind.

The Retreat Programme

It is not complete withdrawal into the relaxation mode because there is work to be done and this is given us by the routine of the day. Eucharist and liturgical prayer, address, and meditation on it, times of relaxation, stillness and contemplation, reading and quiet walks, is the retreat environment in which a further realisation of God as creator and sustainer is experienced. In unhurried attention to God, his glory, his goodness and mercy and will gradually become known. The retreat becomes a deliberate and sustained act of worship, more wholehearted and full than our lives usually give us time for. Sharing in the corporate worship of the Church supports, refreshes, and liberates the individual, feeds his subconscious mind, and disengages him from himself or herself. This attitude of worship leads us to the realisation of God. The routine only creates the conditions. When we face him in this act and attitude of worship we realise him. The nature of silence is more than just physical. Properly understood, it is a spiritual thing, the background of creation. We enter into it as a condition of our renewal. It was St John of the Cross who wrote, 'From all eternity, in silence, God speaks one Word, and that Word is his Son; and it is in silence that we must hear him.'

The Holy Spirit

Our meditations will be upon certain themes presented by the conductor in his addresses. His purpose is to help us to the realisation of God and to lead us into prayer. The meditations in retreat are consciously recognised as including a third, working through both conductor and retreatant; the Holy Spirit. Our meditation therefore includes a willingness to understand and to be changed by the meditation.

Hearing God

Withdrawal, silence and meditation make up the form of our waiting upon God who makes himself heard in four ways; through prayer, hearing the Scriptures, the addresses or the hymns, and by God clearing obstacles to his grace. Prayer is an expression of our thoughts or love towards him, and may be hesitant. In praising God in Christ, we may be led into humility and penitence, and in that experience we remember his love and atonement. This prompts us to rise again in trust, confidence and thankfulness. Our prayer becomes a living experience in him, as God opens our eyes and ears by the hidden movements of his grace. We may start in one place and end up in another with a changed mind. God the Holy Spirit has brought us there in the silence of a still small voice. Maybe it is a direct word to us through his Son, in some text that is read that may be nothing new, but it hits us with a new force and meaning. A phrase in an address or the line of a hymn may be a direct hit from heaven. The truth is, it is. The addresses may bring us to penitence and a desire to confess a sin, the long time obstruction to grace in our hearts. Those words of Christ, *The kingdom of God is at hand, Repent, and believe the Gospel,* become real.

We may not realise that God has spoken or that we have heard and obeyed. We forget what we were, but we have been changed. Only later do we realise that the retreat was the turning point.

The Conductor's Role

The conductor's role is to help the retreatant to a deeper realisation of God. The ordering of the worship, the addresses, the readings, aim to help the retreatant make use of the withdrawal, the silence, and the opportunities for meditation. The conductor must be available for spiritual counsel and hearing confessions.

A programme was sent to the author of a Prayer Creation and Nature Retreat. It started with an introduction to geology and the next day a field trip to look at fossils on the beach. It included an hour standing in a forest while a forester gave a lecture, looking at slides of flowers and butterflies, and the retreatants being saturated with the conductors' knowledge of the natural world with a few environmentally friendly saints thrown in.

The addresses are not primarily to instruct the

retreatant on the conductor's hobbyhorse or specialities, and certainly are not to controvert. They are addressed to the heart rather than being pure speculation for the intellect alone. Devotional addresses instruct in the truths of the Christian faith in an incidental way while instructing in the art of self-knowledge and prayer more directly. Their distinguishing mark is the combining of an appeal to the will by leading into meditation, with the assisting of the development of the retreatant's spiritual life by helping him to pray and see himself or herself as he or she really is.

Their aim is to move the wills of the hearers. 'God's *will* for me' has to be accepted by the *will* of each retreatant. The addresses make real such truths as he already knows; the fundamental truths of the faith that may have been forgotten or prevented from fully motivating his life. Such Christian truths speak to the needs and desires of the retreatants and provide food for meditation. Through his own meditation upon them the retreatant 'realises' God, and in his own meditation afterwards he accepts with his will what God has revealed to him. So the conductor's work is to provide the right material for meditation in an ordered manner, that his hearers may be led into prayer and towards a deepening response to the love of God.

Naturally, the conductor will present what will give retreatants a realisation of God-in-himself, in themes that speak of majesty, eternity, love and the nearness and holiness of God. A conductor must also present to them what will move them to see the bearing of the righteousness of God upon their lives; God's will for them. In his or her bearing, as well as in the words spoken a declaration is being made to the retreatants about what it is to be in retreat, what it is to hear and obey the words, *Be still, and know that I am God.*

There are some worthwhile retreats provided in our Retreat Houses and these are always advertised.

Abuses

Nevertheless, it is important not to debase the word 'retreat' by applying it to other meetings that have other aims and methods. In the present climate this has begun to happen with the contemporary emphasis on the individual in his or her own search for a 'spirituality' (a modern word), that meets their apparent needs.

A flick through a *Retreats Brochure* soon reveals lists of events wrongfully claiming the title 'retreat' and advising that as long as you know your need there is something for everyone. Circular dancing 'retreats' assumes the fixed programme to be inhibiting so everything is optional. The premise is that this is 'their time', for catching up on sleep or talking to another retreatant, or doing their own thing, that is seen not as 'opting out' but as integral to the 'retreat'. Dancing around a candle and aromatic oils, an individual reading his poetry or prose, and when overheated, everyone retiring under a tree to play triangles, drums and tambourines. Worship is a time to experience something different from normal Sunday worship, so liturgies are DIY or culled from elsewhere rather than the Church. 'All the participants were included in the liturgy, rather than having one leader and a passive congregation', and prayers were hung on a growing vine which became the centrepiece around which they all danced until the end of the 'retreat'.

There are workshops on Dreams, Creation Spirituality, Dance, Massage, Transition at Mid-Life. You can have Walking 'Retreats', a 12,000 mile service, an enneagram to link your personality type to the right kind of prayer, the spirituality of travel, and a catering 'retreat' in preparation for Christmas, exploring tasty alternatives to the usual Christmas fare. You might like a 'Quiet Day' looking at birds, butterflies, plants and flowers, a day of t'ai chi or explore your mid-life journey, or learn Gendlin's technique for integrating blocked feelings (must be pre-booked). You may need tools for continuing the Easter Experience or the Forgiving Experience or perhaps you need a reiki day or bio energetics day when the body speaks its mind. You may prefer a Spirituality and Ageing Retreat, Meditation in the context of Psychosynthesis or Meditation and Massage, maybe just the massage. As yet there is no Meditation and Sauna, but there are all the Prayer and ... 'retreats', with all those subjects and activities, including calligraphy, just like the *Teach Yourself Books.*

The Fundamental Error

So many of these so-called 'retreats' are a search for self-transcendence and the enlightenment this brings. Like the stressed-out businessman going into the firm's 'retreat' all he wants to discover is how to cope with his stress. Falling in love with 'spirituality' rather than God is easy, especially when it is tailored to fit 'my apparent needs'. A semi-circle with the closed arc facing upwards illustrates what is happening. The individual is focused on self and his apparent needs rather than on God. 'Spirituality' then becomes a compartment of life and the search to find ways of linking it to our physical environment, rather than what integrates all life. Hence the concern with spiritual traditions and techniques that teach self-transcendence in the face of materialism and self-seeking, the most useful psychological practices and the most helpful beliefs. Whatever provides the most specific guidance will feature more than other spiritual traditions. It is a journey in how to develop, live and grow in a way of self-transcendence and enlightenment. 'Walls' that have hitherto inhibited the flowering of such enlightenment in education and conditioned attitudes towards one's emotions must be demolished. Only then can spiritual enlightenment be nurtured by using techniques of meditation suited to our personality type, dream symbolism, visualisation and self-exploration that lead to enhancement and self-awareness as progress and pitfalls are monitored on the way.

A Grace

This way of enlightenment is more a scientology of self-actualisation, more a psychologism than a 'spirituality'.

Such techniques can increase one's self-knowledge in a way that can be life enhancing, but like Jungian analysis it can only be ancillary to human and spiritual growth and not the heart of it. For Christians the end of human life is more than self-actualisation and is a grace not a technique. Centred in our redemption in Christ, human and spiritual growth is nothing less than a Christian's participation in God's triune life of self-giving love and humility that enables growth in self-control. A retreat is not the search for a technique of 'spirituality' to fit one's needs, but a time for growth in the Christian or baptismal life. This is the fruit of living through Word and Sacrament in Christ with whom the Christian lives in the Father through the Holy Spirit. Here the opening of the semi-circle faces upwards illustrating that the retreatant is focused away from self and completely on God. It is only in God that the Christian discovers the real self and his real needs, and realises that the false self, the self we think we are and its apparent needs, does not exist. Here we open in receptivity and obedience, listening rather than giving, commanding or speaking. It is not a passive condition, but a consciousness; a realisation that our acts do not originate in ourselves but are drawn out and inspired by acts of God. Such inspiration will effect in us a radical change of heart and mind that brings new vision. Yet this will only happen in so far as we are willing to die in order that we might live. For the experience, in so far as nothing is blocking our response cleanses and awakens our adoration and love. Our consciousness is awakened and touched by a living Presence that is spontaneously shared. From this Presence is received an infusion of life that issues spontaneously in thoughts and acts rising from this change of feeling in this communion of prayer.

> Be at peace with your own soul, enter eagerly into the treasure house that is within you and so you will see the things that are in heaven; for there is but one single entry to them both. The ladder that leads to the kingdom is hidden within your soul. Flee from sin, dive into yourself and in your soul you will discover the stairs by which to ascend.
>
> (St Isaac of Nineveh)

Appendix 2

What has happened to Ascetical Theology?

The term 'ascetical theology' seems to have disappeared and with it a concern for the disciplined *ascesis* that must undergird the living of the Christian life. One wonders whether this particular loss is the root cause of the moral confusion in which the Church of England finds itself. F. P. Harton's, *The Elements of the Spiritual Life,* reprinted in 1957, was perhaps the last published Anglican work on ascetical theology. 'Spirituality', a modern word, is the popular term used to describe contemporary preoccupations with what is often termed 'finding a spiritual life', and with it has come an interest in Celtic spirituality, Bendictine spirituality, Carmelite spirituality, Franciscan spirituality et al. The undiscerning see these as entities in themselves and search within them for parallels to our own age. To the more discerning these commendable and authentic styles of Christian living are not 'spiritualities' in themselves, but different ways of living out the only spirituality the Church has, that is Christian spirituality. Often the self-regarding aim and objective of this search for 'a spiritual life' is the acquiring of a measurable 'feel good factor' of renewal, and a 'getting friendly with your emotions' through a self-contained activity with its series of 'spiritual techniques'. Its term of reference has often been the world rather than the Kingdom in the search for relevance. It has thrown up gurus galore.

One is not denigrating the contemporary interest in things 'mystical' and the genuine spiritual thirst and hunger for a life of prayer, but merely flagging a warning about self-appointed gurus who would exploit this present climate of interest and lead people into spiritual cul-de-sacs. In a time of New Age influences, yoga and relaxation classes, the danger of confusing syncretisms happening in 'technique-centred' courses becomes real. Too often when people are excused for their self-indulgent misbehaviour by describing them as only being human, it is a diminished view of being human that is implied; humanity without the deifying effects of life in Christ. There is behind this attitude an underlying expectation that such misbehaviour is necessary to the finding of human fulfilment. With an emphasis on escaping from the unbearable tensions, dangers and sufferings of 'the world of action', true Christian living can be bypassed and the resultant 'spirituality' is no more than a dead pietism that wants to escape the facing of the true self and the world.

Such confusions give the word 'spirituality' an ambiguous use today, so that like the late Orthodox theologian Alexander Schmemann, I prefer using the term 'Christian life'. Life in Christian prayer is nourished by the Word and Sacraments of the Church, where we enter more deeply into the deified humanity of Christ by the Spirit who dwells in us. It is not an escape into another life, a spiritual world, but living the life God has given us, renewed, transformed and transfigured by the Holy Spirit, that we may grow to a Christic dimension of humanity responsible for the whole creation. Here the means and the end of Christian life is the new nature that makes the Christian completely human. With the Ascension the living and life-giving presence of Christ was made available in all places and all times. So the Christian is a temple of the Holy Spirit that flows from the Father through the Son into his creation. Far from delivering us from the stresses and tensions, dangers and sufferings of this present world, it immerses us in them, that through the paschal mystery in which we are caught up they might be redeemed, as we live with Christ in the Father through the Holy Spirit. In the many situations and circumstances where the Christian can penetrate, such as marriage and family life, through the special skills of one's daily work in industry, commerce, agriculture, teaching, law or medicine, the deifying effects of God's presence are brought to bear on his creation by the spirit in which life is lived and the disciplines peculiar to each job and situation are responded to. Thus the Christian's lifestyle is the manner in which lay theology is written.

Ascesis

The underlying principle of the Christian life is not just a matter of continuous prayer. There is need for, to use the technical word, *Ascesis* or *Asceticism,* which literally means training. What the Desert Fathers have to say about this is found in Cassian's XIVth Conference on *Spiritual Knowledge,* and the father with whom he confers is Abbot Nesteros. Here the abbot tells us that Spiritual Knowledge is twofold. First, practical, the aim of which is to effect an improvement of morals and purification from faults, and secondly, theoretical or contemplative, consisting in the contemplation of the things of God and the knowledge of most sacred thoughts.

Anyone who wishes to arrive at the deep knowledge of the things of God and insight, must pursue first with all might and main the improvement of morals and purification of virtues. The practical knowledge can be won without the contemplative, but the contemplative cannot possibly be won without the practical. In other words it is a waste of time for anyone to expect to attain to the vision of God who does not shun every stain of sin. It is the pure in heart and they alone that shall see God.

This practical perfection depends on two things. First, a person must know the nature of his or her faults and the cure for them. Next, he or she must find out the order of the virtues and form his or her character by striving for perfection in them. If we have not understood the nature of our faults or tried to eradicate them, we cannot hope to gain that understanding of the virtues, which is the second stage of our practical training or that insight into heavenly things which is that contemplative knowledge.

This practical training is what we call *ascesis.* It means

the voluntary denial of things, even if intrinsically good, for the sake of a greater union with God. The Desert Fathers were called ascetics because they led an ascetic life that demonstrated the fact that there can be no authentic Christianity without self-denial. The call to repentance in the Gospel implies an ascetic self-denial that is intimately tied up with sin and its roots in us, and our union with God.

Is Asceticism Outmoded Today?

The Second Vatican Council claims that the asceticism practiced by these monks is not outmoded:

> Spiritual life is not solely enclosed within participation in the liturgy ... St Paul exhorts us to bear Jesus' mortification in our body so that the life of Jesus may be manifest in our mortal body. 'Through prayer, example and the *efforts of penance,* the ecclesial community exercises a true mother-hood in order to lead souls to Christ.' Read the *Acts of the Apostles* where the sending of some members in mission is preceded by prayer and fasting done by everyone.

Pope Paul VI said 'A Christian life without a spirit of asceticism cannot maintain itself and persevere in fruitful spiritual richness and as an apostolic testimony.'

In the *ASB* the Collects for Lent remind us of the need for ascetical endeavour. Ash Wednesday prays that God may ... create in us new and contrite hearts, that, lamenting our sins and acknowledging our wretchedness, we may receive from you, the God of all mercy, perfect forgiveness and peace, but note, not before acknowledging the nature of our faults and the cure of them. It continues on Lent 1, where in the spirit of Jesus fasting in the wilderness we pray ... give us grace to discipline ourselves in obedience to your Spirit; and as you know our weakness so may we know your power to save ... Lent 2 continues this same spirit of prayer ... grant your people grace to withstand the temptations of the world, the flesh, and the devil, and with pure hearts and minds to follow you, the only God; but Lent 3 tells us that if we are to follow

God it must be the same way as Jesus, who '. . . went not up to joy before he suffered pain, and entered not into glory before he was crucified; mercifully grant that we, walking in the way of the Cross, may find it none other than the way of life and peace'.

The Ascetical or Practical Life

Ascetical or practical life is not just for monks. Such people can help us grasp something of the spirit and principle of the spiritual life, which is precisely what Cassian grasped from the Desert Fathers. There is no need to live the same kind of life. It can be lived out in varying circumstances among different interests and professions. We must reach perfection in whatever state of life we find ourselves in and to which God calls us, with the grace received. There are many different ways by which people draw nearer to God, but within each way a person must try to grasp this practical or moral discipline without which the contemplative purity necessary to see God will not be attained.

'If any man do His will, he shall know of the doctrine', is the heart of Our Lord's teaching. Cassian stressed the fact that any form of Christian life may provide the exercises necessary to the practice of the Christian virtues. It is possible within the ordinary and commonplace, the daily round and common task. In his hymn *Teach Me My God and King,* George Herbert wrote that it is the presence of God who 'makes drudgery divine'.

If this sounds too negative, we need to remind ourselves that all life has an element of self-denial and that everyone, believer or unbeliever, discovers this. Life would be impossible if we did not acknowledge certain restraints or acts of self-denial. Otherwise we would be slaves to all the instinctual compulsions and whims that blow upon us, and become anti-social without some self-restraint. Today's emphasis on restricting our eating and drinking and abandoning smoking is to safeguard health. Similarly, *we bite our tongues* to save a friendship or safeguard our job. This natural asceticism is part of everyone's life and demonstrates that it is the giving up of something of value to oneself only to acquire something better.

Christian Asceticism

Asceticism is never an end in itself, otherwise it would be a purely negative attitude to life. It is always a means to an end. Christian asceticism while the same in principle to natural asceticism is put into practice for a different reason. It is in order to detach ourselves from, or forsake all that we have, because, if not, *you cannot be my disciple.*

Like those preparing for the London Marathon, their disciplined training detaches them from over-eating and drinking the wrong substances, and produces a fit body and a healthy cardio-vascular system. It is all just a means to an end – so that on the day while they may not win the race, they will finish the course with dignity and expertise.

Our disciplined training is so that we can run the race of the Christian disciple and as the athlete cannot treat his body with contempt, neither does the Christian athlete. We are not to kill our humanity but merely enable the human to grow with and alongside the spiritual that the whole of ourselves, body, mind and spirit might be transfigured in the life we are living with Christ in the Holy Spirit. Like the Desert Fathers who were soaked in the Bible, we must acknowledge that everything God made is good. However, everything, as the Bible reminds us, has fallen into anarchy because of sin. Our concern must be to re-establish some order in our faculties. As in athletic discipline the body is restored to fitness, so through spiritual discipline the body is transformed under the influence of the Holy Spirit. To be a disciple means to take up the Cross given in Baptism and follow Christ and the ascetical discipline is to enable the new life received in Baptism to be fully developed. In this way our whole being is transfigured into the image of the Risen Christ. As the athlete has liberated his body for the marathon so the Christian disciple discovers that the ascetic discipline liberates the whole being in the deepest sense of the word.

It has a purifying effect as it reaches down into the root of our chaotic and disarrayed faculties to attack the self-love, pride and selfishness, enabling the divine charity to overcome these evil influences in us. St Isaac the Syrian used to say 'Love all mortification and your passions will be put down.' In his First Conference with Abbot Moses Cassian records Moses saying that the first thing in all the arts and sciences is to have some goal, a mark for the mind and constant mental purpose because unless a person keeps this before him with all diligence and persistence, he will never succeed in arriving at the ultimate aim and find what he desires. Similarly, the farmer must plan to keep his field free from brambles and weeds (ascetic effort), while his crops are growing and the weeded soil (purity of heart), will produce an abundant harvest (the life of union with God).

In his conference with the Abbot Paphnutius Cassian describes the relationship between three books of Scripture and self-renunciation. There are three sorts of renunciation, Paphnutius told Cassian. The first concerns our detachment from the bodily or material things of this life; the wealth and goods of this world. God called Abraham to do just this and leave his own country. The second kind of detachment necessary in the way of perfection is from kinsfolk. Paphnutius sees this as renunciation from one's former life and habits and sins which cling to us from our very birth by ties of affinity and kinship. The third renunciation for those in Christ is not to regard the things that are seen but the things that are not seen as of eternal value. When this is done our words and actions witness to the fact that, in the words of the apostle, 'our conversation is in heaven'. Paphnutius links these three renunciations to three books of Scripture. Proverbs teaches us how to live an honest life and see the transitoriness of earthly things. Ecclesiastes speaks of vanity, or as we would say, the inadequacy of everything that makes up the present life. Finally, the The Song of Songs demonstrates a soul purified and united to the Word of God already contemplating the realities of heaven.

Printed in the United Kingdom
by Lightning Source UK Ltd.
120793UK00002B/262-279

9 780852 446775